PRESENTED TO

....

BY

....

DATE

....

DEVOTIONS
LIVE WISE
FOR MEN

DEVOTIONS

LIVE WISE

FOR MEN

180 READINGS

BARBOUR
PUBLISHING

ISBN 979-8-89151-180-4

All scripture quotations are taken from the King James Version of the Bible.

Cover design by Greg Jackson, Thinkpen Design

Published by Barbour Publishing, Inc., 1810 Barbour Drive, Uhrichsville, Ohio 44683, www.barbourbooks.com

Our mission is to inspire the world with the life-changing message of the Bible.

Member of the Evangelical Christian Publishers Association

Printed in China.

Happy is the man that findeth wisdom, and the man that getteth understanding.

PROVERBS 3:13

This inspiring 180-entry devotional for men highlights the benefits of living wisely—that is, of living according to God's revealed truth.

Based on the timeless King James Version of scripture, it's packed with insights on the incredible gift of wisdom:

- It belongs to God (Daniel 2:20).
- It is available to us for the asking (James 1:5).
- It is better than any other thing you could desire (Proverbs 8:11).

Live Wise Devotions for Men was written to introduce you to the great wisdom of God found all through scripture. We pray that it will help guide you into your best life.

THE BEGINNING OF KNOWLEDGE

The fear of the LORD is the beginning of knowledge: but fools despise wisdom and instruction.
PROVERBS 1:7

At the heart of the Christian story is relationship. Jesus invites us all into a relationship with God through Himself (John 14:6–7). We experience this relationship through the Holy Spirit. God is ever-present, listening and communicating with us. Today's verse is among the most famous in Proverbs. It also demonstrates the importance of a relationship with God. How? Through "the fear of the LORD."

Many of us were taught as children that fearing God simply means respecting Him. That's a good definition for a child. But fearing God has a richer meaning for adults. Fearing God is trembling awe and hushed reverence. It's not being afraid of God. Rather, fear of the Lord is a crystal-clear acknowledgment that God alone is the all-powerful Creator and Savior.

This is where wisdom begins. The profound recognition that only God sustains your life is the first step to living wisely. And what does God want with you? Relationship—your time, your prayers, your energy, your heart. If you want to live wise, foster your relationship with Him.

Lord, thank You for loving me. I want to live a wise life. Help me to grow a deeper relationship with You.

BLESSINGS IN PERSECUTION

Blessed are they which are persecuted for righteousness' sake: for theirs is the kingdom of heaven.
MATTHEW 5:10

The Bible includes many examples of intense persecution—even martyrdom—of God's people. The Old Testament prophets were persecuted and so were those who preached the gospel during New Testament times. This is in keeping with these words of the apostle Paul: "All that will live godly in Christ Jesus shall suffer persecution" (2 Timothy 3:12).

Jesus very clearly taught that living for Him wouldn't always be easy. There would be times when those who faithfully followed Him would face all sorts of opposition and persecution. After promising God's blessings for doing this, He went on to say, "Blessed are ye, when men shall revile you, and persecute you, and shall say all manner of evil against you falsely, for my sake. Rejoice, and be exceeding glad: for great is your reward in heaven: for so persecuted they the prophets which were before you" (Matthew 5:11–12).

Persecution and opposition were a part of the lives of God's people in biblical times, and they will be for you today. But when it happens, you can thank God, knowing that He will surely bless you.

Jesus, thank You for the blessings You bring me when I face opposition or persecution.

THE VERY BAD TRADE

And he said, I heard thy voice in the garden,
and I was afraid. . .and I hid myself.
GENESIS 3:10

Did you read the word *wisdom* in today's verse? No? Well, it's because it isn't there. So why talk about something that isn't intentionally wise in a book about wisdom? Well, you need to know there's a very bad trade that many people willingly make. They trade wisdom for knowledge. Adam did this. You probably have too.

Wisdom is a good gift from a good God. He gave Adam and his wife Eve all that they would need so they could do the right thing. The first two humans were created with the ability to remain sinless. They had one rule but chose to break it. Why? Breaking this rule promised knowledge. They believed this defiant move would make them like God, but by trading wisdom for knowledge they discovered something they'd never experienced before—fear.

Their choice to embrace knowledge placed a barrier between themselves and God and it was a fearful thing. Of course God had a plan to manage man's lawbreaking through His Son, Jesus, but when knowledge made Adam afraid perhaps he and his wife remembered that God's wisdom had always inspired trust and confidence. The first two humans lost both.

I'm not interested in being afraid, God.
Help me trust You, resist fear, and embrace wisdom
today, tomorrow, and every day of my life.

CONTINUE STEADFASTLY

And they continued stedfastly in the apostles' doctrine and fellowship, and in breaking of bread, and in prayers.

ACTS 2:42

On the Day of Pentecost, a group of Christians (maybe the 120 mentioned in Acts 1:15) were gathered in a house, and the Holy Spirit filled them. When Jews from every nation heard these new converts speaking to them in their own language, some of them suspected these new Christians were drunk with wine. But Peter stood—full of power from the Holy Spirit—and preached his first sermon, assuring the crowd that these men weren't drunk but rather, filled with the Spirit of God. His impassioned plea led to the salvation of three thousand people that day.

They continued steadfastly in fellowship with one another, adhering to what the apostles taught them, breaking of bread, and praying. Just as this was important for first-century believers, it's still one of the best ways to stay on fire for Christ. The wise Christian doesn't try to survive alone, for he knows Satan is roaming about, looking for those he may devour. Often, those are Christians who have strayed from fellowship, beyond the protective fold that Christ offers to His church.

Lord, when I desire to pull away from fellowship with other believers, remind me that I need the protective covering of Your church.

DAY-AND-NIGHT DELIGHT

Blessed is the man that walketh not in the counsel of the ungodly, nor standeth in the way of sinners, nor sitteth in the seat of the scornful. But his delight is in the law of the LORD; and in his law doth he meditate day and night.

PSALM 1:1–2

The book of Psalms is an amazing compilation of wisdom. While the Psalter is largely a collection of corporate worship songs, there's a remarkable array of topics discussed—everything from the universal (for example, creation) to the deeply personal (for example, lust).

But it's not coincidental that the ancient Jewish scribes who arranged the book began with Psalm 1, specifically verses 1–2. These verses serve as a framework for the rest of the collection—and indeed, our very lives as followers of Christ.

Just like the Psalter itself, true human wisdom begins with our "delight. . .in the law of the LORD" (Psalm 1:2). Think about your life before you came to love God's Word. Were your decisions wise? Were they done in humility and self-sacrifice? Did they have eternal value? Did they please your Creator?

Without God's law being written on our hearts (Proverbs 7:3), we can never have true wisdom. Seek the law of the Lord. Meditate on it every day. This is where eternal wisdom is found.

Lord, I want to delight in Your Word. Help me to meditate on it day and night.

WISDOM WITHOUT CREDENTIALS

When the sabbath day was come, [Jesus] began to teach in the synagogue: and many hearing him were astonished, saying, From whence hath this man these things? and what wisdom is this which is given unto him, that even such mighty works are wrought by his hands?

MARK 6:2

Meeting Jesus when He was on earth must have been impressive, but with a dash of confusion thrown in. Now it wouldn't be Jesus who confuses, but His actions, words, and thoughts meant that people were considering ideas that seemed—impossible.

His wisdom gave Him powerful words to speak to the lost and hurting as well as those with pride and influence. Some were offended by His wise words.

Jesus spoke in the synagogue, a Jewish worship center. His teaching exceeded that of anyone they'd ever heard. This was the impressive part. But Jesus came from a poor family and had no formal training. That was the confusing part. This man who had no accepted credentials was speaking with power, healing with compassion, and teaching with encouragement. This seemed impossible to the crowd, but then again, the wisdom Jesus brought also delivered miracles, life, and rescue.

Don't be confused—be impressed.

Let me be impressed by You, Father. I don't want to be confused by refusing to believe that You're wise enough to make impossible things possible.

THE WISEST MAN ON EARTH

The LORD gave Solomon wisdom, as he promised him.

1 KINGS 5:12

King David's son Solomon was chosen to be the new king of Israel. God did something remarkable for him: He invited Solomon to ask for something he really wanted. Maybe thoughts of riches or fame were tempting to consider, but Solomon made *wisdom* his first choice.

The practical reason Solomon chose this gift? He'd never led a nation before. If he was going to do so with confidence he needed wisdom more than anything else. That choice led to a reign that was remarkable for great decisions. He became the wisest man on earth.

It can be hard to determine the value we should place on wisdom. It doesn't seem as important as money in a bank account or a name everyone recognizes. But a unique thing happened when Solomon asked for wisdom: Yes, he was given the ability to understand hard things and deal with difficult situations, but God also gave him riches and honor among people throughout the world.

The pursuit of wisdom leads to opportunity for impact. This didn't escape the notice of the God who wants to give wisdom.

Give me a heart to pursue wisdom, Lord. Make this a primary pursuit once I accept Your rescue plan. Help me to know You, understand Your Word, and be willing to follow You every day from now until eternity.

LOVE: THE PROPER MOTIVATION

If ye love me, keep my commandments.
JOHN 14:15

Sadly, many Christian men attempt to obey Christ's commands out of a sense of fear—fear that they will lose their place in His eternal kingdom or fear that they will miss out on the blessings He has for them.

That never works out well.

After demonstrating His love for His disciples by humbly washing their feet, Jesus commanded them to follow His example by washing one another's feet (John 13:14–15) and by loving one another as He had loved them (13:34). He urged them to put their unwavering faith in God the Father and the Son (14:1).

Then, before promising to send the Holy Spirit, Jesus told them, "If you love me, keep my commandments." Jesus wanted His disciples—and us today—to understand that the motivation of everything done for Him should not be fear or the desire for God's blessing, but love.

The apostle John later wrote, "For this is the love of God, that we keep his commandments: and his commandments are not grievous" (1 John 5:3). In other words, if you love God, you'll obey His commandments with a willing, joyful heart.

Jesus, You have called me to obey Your commandments, not out of a sense of duty or fear but out of a heart of love for You. Help me to grow in my love for You so that I can also grow in my obedience to Your commandments.

SURVIVORS OF THE STRUGGLE

Take you wise men, and understanding, and known among your tribes, and I will make them rulers over you.
DEUTERONOMY 1:13

It just makes sense that the person who could identify wise men would be another wise man. Maybe that's why Moses chose to populate positions of leadership with wise men who could help lead the people in all the best ways.

It was becoming harder for Moses to provide total leadership for all the people who'd vacated Egypt in favor of journeying to the new land God promised. These men would have been former slaves who suffered the abuse of those who were over them. They'd been chased by men who really didn't want them to leave. They'd lived through struggle in a wilderness expedition with which others found fault. Somewhere among all the grumblers were men who were wise. They resisted the wayward tendencies that claimed so many of the wandering people.

These men became the leaders the people needed. They helped Moses as they collectively followed God.

Having a difficult life doesn't automatically make you wise. But if you survive a struggle by keeping your focus on God, you can't help but come out better.

Lord, please make my struggles valuable by causing me to gain wisdom through them. I know that You use hardship as discipline in Your children's lives.

DO YOUR PART

But ye, beloved, building up yourselves on your most holy faith, praying in the Holy Ghost, keep yourselves in the love of God, looking for the mercy of our Lord Jesus Christ unto eternal life.

JUDE 20–21

As false teachers infiltrated the church, Jude issued a warning in his short letter against apostasy. He urged believers to remain faithful while helping other believers to do the same. In today's scripture, he offers four key elements in remaining faithful.

First, build up yourselves on the most holy faith—this implies it is the believer's responsibility to do so. Second, pray in the Holy Ghost—a reference to being open to the Spirit's guidance and seeking personal alignment with God's will. Third, keep yourselves in the love of God—which involves obeying His commands and cultivating a deep, personal relationship with Him, in Christ. And fourth, look for the mercy of Christ to eternal life—this means living with the awareness of eternity, trusting in the finished work of Christ for salvation.

As you engage in all four activities, the Holy Spirit will enable you to spot false teachers and fend off untruths that the world wants you to believe.

Father, I want to go deeper with You—so deep that I'll never fall for any lies that this world offers.

BEING A WISE FRIEND

Iron sharpeneth iron; so a man sharpeneth the countenance of his friend.
PROVERBS 27:17

Take a look at the knife block in your kitchen. Chef's knife. Paring knife. Steak knives. Serrated knives. Maybe a pair of scissors. . .and even a sharpening rod. If you've ever used that rod, you've probably learned that sharpening a knife means more than just making the edge finer. Sharpening a knife straightens out the blade. The rod flattens nicks and reshapes curves in the metal. It points the blade in the right direction.

Friends need each other to stay pointed in the right direction. Wise friends help us navigate both good and bad days well. Within the context of Proverbs, friends encourage each other to seek knowledge and fear the Lord (Proverbs 1:7). There is also a time and place for thoughtful correction when necessary (Proverbs 27:5; 15:23).

But there's even more to unpack here. The two friends are both iron. They're the same material, presented equally. You are brothers in the family of God. So, sharpen your friends with humility and love, and allow them to sharpen you too. Set aside time to develop authentic friendships with faithful, Christian men in your community. God often uses Christian friendships to point people in the right direction.

Lord, I want to be a wise friend.
Help me to foster friendships that please You.

AN UNASHAMED WORKMAN

Study to shew thyself approved unto God, a workman that needeth not to be ashamed, rightly dividing the word of truth.
2 TIMOTHY 2:15

Today's verse is written to Timothy, a pastor. Paul wanted his young charge to make sure he was studying the Word of God in such a way as to be approved unto God—in other words, not to please people by tickling their ears with teaching they want to hear. Much has been said about rightly dividing the Word of truth. Bible commentator Matthew Henry wrote this: "Not to invent a new gospel, but rightly to divide the gospel that is committed to their trust. To speak terror to those to whom terror belongs, comfort to whom comfort; to give every one *his portion in due season.*"

While today's passage is written to a pastor, it's not a stretch to say it applies to all believers. We study the scriptures because we earnestly desire to see others come to faith in Christ, and the rightly divided Word of God fills our spiritual wells. You have many tools at your disposal to help you rightly divide the Word—Bible commentaries, Bible dictionaries, and concordances. If you aren't sure how to use them, ask a more seasoned believer. He'll be glad to help you.

Lord, I want to go deeper into Your Word. Help me to study to show myself approved unto You.

FAMILIES DEFINED BY WISDOM

And of the children of Issachar, which were men that had understanding of the times, to know what Israel ought to do; the heads of them were two hundred; and all their brethren were at their commandment.

1 Chronicles 12:32

Imagine an entire family known for wisdom. This describes the family of Issachar, a tribe in Israel. There probably were exceptions, but most of these men were relied upon because they had insight into good decision-making. They put the puzzle pieces together in a way that brought about positive outcomes.

These were men of conviction and purpose. And there was an organization to the way they did things too. Two hundred were leaders and everyone else was committed to doing what these leaders asked. True wisdom comes from God, and it informed these men's effort. That explains why their wisdom was sought by others.

Imagine your family and what it would be like to have it defined by wisdom, conviction, and purpose. Someone would need to lead, and others would need to follow. The wisdom would have to come from God. If that sounds too good to be true, remember the tribe of Issachar.

I would love to choose wisdom, God. I would love for my family to choose wisdom. You've given so many gifts but could we also have the gift of wisdom?

BEING "GOLDEN"

And as ye would that men should do to you, do ye also to them likewise.
LUKE 6:31

Most everyone likes to receive good from someone else. We appreciate when a friend comes through for us in a pinch—say when we need help moving or repairing our car. We like it when someone takes the time to call or text us when we're in a tough spot and need a simple word of encouragement.

Can you relate?

In the above verse, Jesus turns things around a bit when He encourages us to be *that* man—the one who goes out of his way to do for others the things he'd like people to do for him. Jesus' words have come to be known as the "Golden Rule."

But notice what Jesus *didn't* say: He didn't teach that we Christians should do good for others with the expectation that they would reciprocate. He didn't teach that people, out of the goodness of their hearts, would do good for you simply because you've done good for them.

It's both wise and loving to be on the lookout for opportunities to bless others—just because.

Jesus, help me to always seek out opportunities to do for others the things I'd like them to do for me—and then follow through.

UNSETTLED

Thou wilt keep him in perfect peace, whose mind is stayed on thee: because he trusteth in thee.

Isaiah 26:3

Feeling a little restless? Does it sometimes seem as if no matter what you do and what you may choose you're a bit unsettled? Of course it does. Everyone seems to live in this unsettled place. Discontent is a companion you may struggle to get rid of. Anything resembling peace is elusive.

What you think about has a great impact on how you feel and the way you respond to difficulties. Fear removes peace because you're focused more on problems than on the God who can help you work through your issues. The trust that rightfully belongs to God is often placed in your own efforts, which ultimately proves faulty. This is a path that reduces trust, brings discontent, and looks nothing like wisdom.

To get out of this unsettled place, engage your mind. You have the responsibility to stay, fix, and lock your thoughts onto God. He is trustworthy, and when you remind yourself of that over and over again, as often as it takes to find peace, you will. And God's peace is perfect.

Thank You for Your peace, Lord. I know it's wise to trade my fear for Your peace. Please help me to do that.

THE POWER OF GOD

That your faith should not stand in the wisdom of men, but in the power of God.
1 CORINTHIANS 2:5

To the unbeliever, Christianity doesn't make sense. To find life, we must lose it (Matthew 16:25). To become great, we must become servants (Matthew 23:11). Strength is found in weakness (2 Corinthians 12:9). To be exalted, we must humble ourselves (James 4:10). We are made rich by becoming poor (2 Corinthians 8:9). Freedom is found in becoming a servant of Christ (Romans 6:22). To be wise, we must become foolish in the eyes of the world (1 Corinthians 3:18). Victory comes through surrender (Romans 12:1). We find true joy by enduring trials (James 1:2).

When the world tells you that you're on the wrong track, it's a good indicator that you are on the right one. Do not rest in the wisdom of men but rather, in the power of God, for He is the author of wisdom (Daniel 2:20, Proverbs 2:6, James 1:5). On the other hand, the wisdom of this world is perishing: "For it is written, I will destroy the wisdom of the wise, and will bring to nothing the understanding of the prudent" (1 Corinthians 1:19).

Father, I choose this day to rest my faith in Your power. You are the author of wisdom. Why would I turn to the foolishness of this world?

PLACE OF REFUGE

I will say of the L*ORD*, *He is my refuge and my fortress: my God; in him will I trust.*

Psalm 91:2

In cases of premeditated homicide in ancient Israel, Old Testament law allowed for a male relative of the slain individual to exact revenge on the murderer. But as God was bringing Israel into the Promised Land, He commanded the Israelites to set up six "cities of refuge" spread throughout the land (Numbers 35). These cities were to be safe havens for someone who had accidentally killed another. Within the cities of refuge, those guilty of manslaughter could go to trial to prove their innocence from murder while avoiding the wrath of the avenger.

When the Old Testament's original Jewish readers read verses like Psalm 91:2, the term *refuge* would have brought to mind very real images of safety from impending danger.

In this fallen world, we live outside the city walls. Dangers—spiritual and otherwise—are everywhere. Trials and hardships frequently arrive at our doorstep. Yet God is a very real refuge. We can run to Him in our times of trouble. Through scripture, prayer, and fellowship with other believers, we can flee into the safety of His presence. As Psalm 46:1 affirms, "God is our refuge and strength, a very present help in trouble."

God, thank You for being my refuge during the trials of life. Help me run to You for safety and strength.

THE GRACE OF FORGIVENESS

In whom we have redemption through his blood, the forgiveness of sins, according to the riches of his grace; wherein he hath abounded toward us in all wisdom and prudence.

Ephesians 1:7–8

God created a plan of salvation that involved His Son: Jesus would die for the laws you've broken, He would come back to life to defeat death, and He would live to help you learn how these truths impact your life.

The grace God gives is an indicator that there are things we don't deserve. Consider the gift of forgiveness. The applicable links to this are as follows: We were given rules to follow. . .we either ignored the rules or chose to break them. . .we're now guilty of breaking His rules. . .in His grace God gives us something we don't deserve: forgiveness.

Now, you need to ask yourself if you follow the same set of grace links. Do you give the grace of forgiveness? Have you accepted this kind of wisdom?

The wisdom God provides will help you make choices that make sense to Him, even if not always to you. And in the end, He's the one who truly matters.

If grace has a heartbeat then it's living wisdom, Father. May I accept Your forgiveness and then be wise enough to follow Your example as I forgive others—even those who've hurt me badly.

THE PURSUIT OF HAPPINESS

Happy is the man that findeth wisdom,
and the man that getteth understanding.
PROVERBS 3:13

The United States was founded, in large part, on "the pursuit of Happiness." That's a direct quote from the Declaration of Independence, one of the "certain unalienable Rights" with which men are "endowed by their Creator." The question is, how do you catch the happiness you're pursuing?

In our world, many people chase happiness through wealth or notoriety or sex or some other selfish pursuit. Others do good things, hoping that service to their fellow man might lead to fulfillment. Any of these things can produce happiness, at least in the moment. But God's Word shows us the formula for ultimate, long-lasting happiness: Find wisdom, get understanding.

How? Well, wisdom and understanding come from God and His Word. The text leading up to today's scripture tells us to "forget not my law" (verse 1); "let not mercy and truth forsake thee" (verse 3); "trust in the LORD with all thine heart" (verse 5); "honour the LORD with thy substance" (verse 9); and "despise not the chastening of the LORD" (verse 11). Wisdom—and ultimate happiness—always arise from our wise and joyful Lord.

Never be "wise in thine own eyes" (Proverbs 3:7). Your goal, as that verse concludes, is to "fear the LORD, and depart from evil." This is not only the pursuit but the finding of happiness.

I want to be happy, Lord. Lead me to Your wisdom.

COMPARATIVELY SPEAKING

Who is a wise man and endued with knowledge among you? let him shew out of a good conversation his works with meekness of wisdom.

James 3:13

Does wisdom need superhero status? Probably not. Wisdom is often quiet and humble. Its strength doesn't have to be in an outward display of force. It arrives at unexpected times with a perfect word that halts poor judgment and suggests a better way. Wisdom is a friend—not a manipulator. It offers insight so the one possessing it can make the better choice.

The things a wise man does won't bear a resemblance to all the foolish things you've seen others do. A wise man may not be perfect (take David and Solomon for instance), but he is always aware of the direction he should walk. And he moves back to wisdom's trail as quickly as possible after straying.

A wise man isn't afraid to speak truth. But he's not interested in trash talking those who insist on proving themselves foolish. The know-it-alls see wisdom as foolishness while the wise will see the know-it-all as someone needing to learn something new.

When I want to prove I'm the smartest man in the room, keep my lips sealed, Father. Help me to wait for Your guidance to share what You want me to share and do what You want me to do.

EAT YOUR WORDS

Death and life are in the power of the tongue:
and they that love it shall eat the fruit thereof.
PROVERBS 18:21

Proverbs are meant to be chewed on. God gave us these short, thoughtful statements to turn over and over in our minds, like a piece of mental bubble gum, allowing the flavor of their wisdom to seep in over a period of time.

The first half of Proverbs 18:21 is clear upon the first bite. Words are *powerful.* A hurtful comment from a loved one can alter the very course of one's life. But so can encouragement from a friend. The man who lives wisely is the man who speaks life to those around him.

The remainder of Proverbs 18:21, though, provides more to chew on. Scripture has much to say about those who love their tongue and enjoy hearing themselves talk. They will eat the empty fruit of destruction (Proverbs 13:3; 29:20). But those who love their tongue in a different sense—by taming it (James 3:6–10)—will use it to say praiseworthy things and ultimately find peace (Philippians 4:8–9).

However you chew on it, the wisdom in this verse can be summed up by saying this: For better or worse, you will eat your words. How do you want them to taste?

Lord, forgive me for sometimes dishonoring You and others with my words. May my speech always be marked by purity and praise.

WISDOM'S CORE

This I pray, that your love may abound yet more and more in knowledge and in all judgment.
PHILIPPIANS 1:9

The greatest choice of wisdom is love. This isn't a kind of love that's simply emotional. You see, at its core, love is a choice. Wisdom understands the difference and makes the choice to love using action instead of words alone.

The apostle Paul indicated that for love to grow, wisdom and understanding must be an important part of the equation. A wise person loves others and that love continues to grow. A key reason for this is that when people recognize love, they want to get close to that level of acceptance. The experience begins with the wisdom of God revealed in John 3:16, which says that He loved the world. He proved that love with the sacrifice of His Son for the sins of mankind. In His wisdom God understood that without this level of love, mankind would be lost.

God wants you to understand that this level of love can be the difference between friendship and loneliness, abandonment and acceptance, or drifting and purpose.

Lord God, You want me to love You and then love everyone else. I know this is wisdom because it reflects why You made me and why You've always wanted a friendship with me.

NONTRANSFERABLE WEALTH

For he seeth that wise men die, likewise the fool and the brutish person perish, and leave their wealth to others.
Psalm 49:10

You can't take it with you.

It's an axiom that we've all heard many times. We mentally assent to it. We nod when the preacher reminds us of this truth.

Yet earthly wealth and possessions continue to lure and ensnare our hearts—quite easily, as a matter of fact.

God knows this. So He filled His Word with reminders to avoid the love of money. In fact, few topics are covered more extensively in scripture than earthly riches.

Psalm 49 reminds us that when the rich die, they meet the same end as the senseless person or the person living in squalor. Ultimately, their riches account for nothing. No one can transfer anything material from this world into eternity.

The wise man truly understands this. The godly man accepts this. The mature follower of Christ lives as he truly is—a temporary steward of God's heavenly largesse.

"Every good gift and every perfect gift is from above, and cometh down from the Father of lights" (James 1:17). Nothing we have, whether it's a half-empty piggy bank or a seven-figure stock portfolio, is truly ours.

We would all be wise to live with this in mind.

God, all I have is truly Yours. Help me to be generous with the gifts You've given to me.

A NEW MIND

And be not conformed to this world: but be ye transformed by the renewing of your mind, that ye may prove what is that good, and acceptable, and perfect, will of God.
Romans 12:2

The world tries to pull you in many directions. It's telling you to climb the corporate ladder, to pursue material wealth and possessions, to follow your own heart, to prioritize your personal happiness, and to chase your dreams. But these endeavors are the desires of a mind that has not been transformed by Christ. Only a transformed mind can determine what is the good, and acceptable, and perfect, will of God.

The Bible has much to say about how a Christian can renew his mind. You can hide the Word in your heart that you might not sin against God (Psalm 119:11). You can practice obedience to God's commands (James 1:22). You can avoid anxiety by praying about every situation (Philippians 4:6–7). You can focus on godly thoughts (Philippians 4:8). You can engage in corporate worship and fellowship (Hebrews 10:24–25). You can love the Lord your God more than the world (1 John 2:15). And you can cultivate the fruit of the Spirit (Galatians 5:22–23).

As you are active with your faith, putting scriptural principles into practice, the Holy Spirit will renew your mind, changing your desires from worldly pursuits to godly ones.

Father, I look forward to a renewed mind as I practice these scriptural admonitions.

MIRTH AND DEATH

The heart of the wise is in the house of mourning;
but the heart of fools is in the house of mirth.
Ecclesiastes 7:4

Take the time to read Ecclesiastes 7:4 again. Does it seem like wisdom is preferred over foolishness? Foolishness seems to be filled with fun and games while wisdom appears to be in the permanent presence of grief.

Perhaps it will make sense to look at wisdom in a different way. When you were a child it was reasonable to expect the actions of a child. . .but growing up likely meant a difference in the way you act, think, and speak.

If all you pursue are things that amuse you then you'll be too busy being amused to have time for the things that could make you wise.

Perhaps Solomon described wisdom alongside grief because wisdom pays attention to the hurt around it. When you're wise, you can't help but feel grief for those who've spent far too long amusing themselves to a place approaching death.

Unwise people pursue mirth to their own harm. Wisdom doesn't ignore that fact.

Lord God, at times I would rather search for amusement than notice the hurt around me. Help me to realize I can never become wise if I don't recognize that all people experience pain.

LIFT UP JESUS

And as Moses lifted up the serpent in the wilderness, even so must the Son of man be lifted up: that whosoever believeth in him should not perish, but have eternal life.

JOHN 3:14–15

Numbers 21 tells the story of God sending venomous snakes as punishment for the Israelites' complaining and unbelief. When Moses prayed for the people, God commanded him to fashion a bronze serpent and place it atop a long pole. The people could look on the snake image and live.

The Israelites couldn't be saved by killing the snakes—only an unusual provision from God Himself gave them any hope of escaping death. The same is true for sinful mankind even today. No one can be saved from the consequences of sin through any self-effort of good works or vows to behave better. All men are saved by looking to God's perfect sin sacrifice: Jesus, who was lifted up on a cross so that all who looked to Him in faith could live eternally.

You've looked up to Jesus for your salvation, so now you have a permanent place in God's eternal kingdom. Now, your responsibility—and privilege—is to lift up Jesus every day so that those around you might be saved when they see and believe.

Jesus, thank You for allowing Yourself to be lifted up on the cross. When men look up to You, they can be saved from the consequences of their sin. May many look to You today.

AN EXISTENTIAL QUESTION

The fool hath said in his heart, There is no God. They are corrupt, they have done abominable works, there is none that doeth good.

Psalm 14:1

For most of human history, the existence of a divine being (or group of gods) was a given in every civilization. From the monotheistic Jews to the ancient Egyptians, whose pantheon of gods numbered two thousand or more, all people groups generally agreed on the existence of some sort of higher power that created and ruled the universe.

That is, until the Age of Enlightenment.

Starting in the seventeenth century, significant leaps forward in science, medicine, and technology gave rise to a new wave of humanistic thinking, devoid of acknowledging either the existence of a deity or at least its active presence.

Yet as Psalm 14:1 affirms, atheism is the epitome of human foolishness. And agnosticism is a closely related cousin. True wisdom doesn't lie in the greater advances of humanity. It begins with the declaration that there is someone greater than us—a Creator God who rules everything He made, fashioned us in His own image, and expects us to worship Him. To truly be wise, we must confess and believe what scripture, the universe itself, and our own consciences all attest to: There is a God, and He is worthy of praise.

God, I believe in You and Your Son. Increase my faith!

FAINT NOT

And let us not be weary in well doing: for in due season we shall reap, if we faint not.
GALATIANS 6:9

Imagine putting in weeks or months on a project at work without ever receiving any accolades from your boss. You put your heart and soul into the job, knowing it would be a product your company could be proud of, one that would really meet the needs of your customers. Just a little acknowledgment would go a long way. But without that recognition, you might "be weary in well doing."

That can happen in the Christian life too. We live for God, trying to honor Him in all we do. But when the world—sometimes even people we know and love—question or mock us, we get weary of doing the right thing. But faithful Christians aren't living to please other people.

Galatians 6:8 gives the context of why we should stay the course: "For he that soweth to his flesh shall of the flesh reap corruption; but he that soweth to the Spirit shall of the Spirit reap life everlasting." We are living with eternity in mind. As we are faithful, we shall reap rewards in due season, if we faint not.

Father, give me the power and strength to stay the course. No matter what anybody says or does to me, I never want to grow weary of doing good for Your glory.

WISDOM IS OBEYING

Abraham. . .rose up, and went unto the place of which God had told him.
GENESIS 22:3

God gave Abraham some very specific, but odd, direction. It involved travel, a sacrifice, and what appeared to be a broken promise.

Would Abraham summon the courage to follow the instructions? Yes. God told this man to sacrifice his son, and Abraham proved willing to do what the Lord asked. When God saw the commitment of Abraham, He rescued the boy—and provided an animal substitute for the sacrifice. Abraham was wise enough to know that, above all, God could be trusted.

It can be hard to read this part of Abraham's story. We wonder why God would ask something so challenging. But sacrifice was something God was planning to do Himself, for all mankind. God the Father would give up His Son, Jesus, to pay the price for the moral laws that every man breaks. Abraham's story is a vivid picture of the price God was willing to pay to rescue someone like you.

Abraham was wise to obey God, even when the command went against every "reasonable" human expectation. Abraham played his part in God's greater plan, and now you are wise to accept the salvation Jesus provided.

I'm overwhelmed by the trust needed to follow You, Lord. Give me the wisdom to embrace trust and the courage to walk with You on difficult assignments.

THE KNOWLEDGE OF HIS WILL

For this cause we also, since the day we heard it, do not cease to pray for you, and to desire that ye might be filled with the knowledge of his will in all wisdom and spiritual understanding; that ye might walk worthy of the Lord unto all pleasing, being fruitful in every good work, and increasing in the knowledge of God.

Colossians 1:9–10

If you want to know what God wants you to do then you'll need "the knowledge of his will." You'll need people praying with and for you. You'll need spiritual understanding. You'll need to grow up.

That isn't a statement of condemnation—it's the description of a rite of passage in your spiritual journey. It's easier to do the wrong thing when you lack God's wisdom to guide you toward the plans that He has for you. Without knowledge of God's will you cannot fulfill the very things He desires. Without wisdom you don't get to participate in His plans because you don't even understand what those plans are.

The pursuit of "the knowledge of his will" makes God happy, improves your spiritual growth, and impacts the world around you.

Lord God, please give me—and the people I care for most—the gift of understanding who You are. Let us all know that You have a plan for our lives, and that we can use Your wisdom to gain the knowledge of Your will.

HEALTHY FEAR

The fear of the LORD is the beginning of wisdom: a good understanding have all they that do his commandments: his praise endureth for ever.

PSALM 111:10

We teach our kids not to be afraid of the dark. We love action movies where the hero shows no fear. Throughout scripture, fear is discouraged as being the opposite of faith.

In Joshua 1:9, God commanded Joshua, "Be not afraid, neither be thou dismayed." In Isaiah 41:10, God tells Israel, "Fear thou not; for I am with thee: be not dismayed; for I am thy God." Elsewhere, God tells Abraham, Gideon, Daniel, and others to "fear not."

So what, then, are we to make of Psalm 111:10, which tells us that wisdom begins with fear? Is scripture contradicting itself? Of course not.

Biblically defined, "the fear of the LORD" refers to approaching Him in reverent awe and wonder, giving Him His due as our Creator, Savior, and King. Those who reject God have much reason to be terrified of His righteous judgment. But all His redeemed children have nothing to fear thanks to Jesus, who has brokered peace between us and a holy God (Romans 5:1). We are now clothed in His righteousness (Isaiah 61:10). This allows us to "come boldly unto the throne of grace" (Hebrews 4:16).

Indeed, the fear of the Lord is the beginning of wisdom!

God, help me worship You in reverent, grateful fear and awe for Your goodness, mercy, and love toward me.

FORGIVENESS IS ALWAYS WISE

For if ye forgive men their trespasses,
your heavenly Father will also forgive you.
MATTHEW 6:14

If we're honest with ourselves, we have to admit that it's tough to always be willing to forgive a person who's done us wrong. But Matthew 6:14—containing words from the mouth of Jesus Himself—tells us there forgiveness is not optional.

As you read that verse, did anyone in particular come to mind? Is there an offense, perhaps many years ago, that still eats at you? Sound biblical wisdom demands that you seek God's help in forgiving that person and moving on from the situation.

Forgiveness matters to God, so much that He sent Jesus to earth to die a sacrificial death so that we all could be forgiven for our sins. Jesus taught that this forgiving, merciful God requires His people to forgive others when they say and do things to offend us.

God wants to make you more and more like Jesus every day. When you choose to forgive others for the wrongs they've done, you become more like your Savior. And that is a wise thing to do.

Lord Jesus, I didn't deserve it, but You made a way for me to be forgiven of even my worst sins. Remind me often that You want me to forgive others, even when they don't deserve it.

NO PRIDE IN WISDOM

Thus saith the Lord, Let not the wise man glory in his wisdom.
Jeremiah 9:23

Someone who simply knows things likes to prove he's the smartest man in the room. But that's not true of someone who's *wise*. True wisdom prevents a man from showing off. Knowledge seeks to impress, while wisdom is inspired to help. Knowledge welcomes pride, but wisdom is embraced by humility. Knowledge seeks a large audience while wisdom seeks an audience of just one—God.

The wise don't seek the limelight and may never find themselves basking in its glow. Wisdom might be found in a backyard swing, a long-term care facility, or among youth on high school and college campuses. Wisdom isn't an age, a look, or a gender. It's a pursuit that starts very personally and is often shared individually.

Wisdom doesn't need a press release, a schedule of interviews, or a podcast in order to flourish. But is is sought when nothing else is making sense. Wisdom is desired when people are only hearing rehearsed answers to complex questions. Mix basic knowledge with godly understanding to get something both rare and priceless—wisdom. Pride and applause are not required.

Lord, I thank You for separating pride from wisdom. This helps me to know what to look for—and what to avoid.

WALK DILIGENTLY

See then that ye walk circumspectly, not as fools,
but as wise, redeeming the time, because the days are evil.
Ephesians 5:15–16

In America, life expectancy is 76.4 years. If you're 20, that sounds like a long time. If you're 73, not so much. That goes hand in hand with what James 4:14 says: "For what is your life? It is even a vapour, that appeareth for a little time, and then vanisheth away."

The Christian doesn't need to fear death, of course. To be absent from the body is to be present with the Lord (2 Corinthians 5:8). Even so, the admonition in today's verses is to make sure you don't spend your life on things that don't matter.

The apostle Paul tells the Ephesian church to walk "circumspectly." The Greek word used here means diligently or perfectly. Bible commentator Adam Clarke makes this point: "Our word *circumspect*, from the Latin *circirmspicio*, signifies to look round about on all hands; to be every way watchful, wary, and cautious, in order to avoid danger." The Christian is to redeem his time. In other words, mindful to buy up moments others might spend more frivolously.

Monitor your time closely this week. Maybe even keep a log of your activities. Then prayerfully review it, asking God to make you more diligent with your time going forward.

Lord God, lead and guide me as I seek to be a better steward of the time You've given me.

THE DIVINE REBOOT

Noah found grace in the eyes of the Lord.
Genesis 6:8

If you try to live by God's principles, it can feel like you're the only one. And Satan uses this feeling to convince you to give up your journey with God. But even if you feel like your best efforts are failing, you've never been alone. Not only does God Himself help you, there are others around who follow God and will contribute to your success.

Noah had only his immediate family to rely on. Every other human he encountered had chosen to reject God. Some of them probably even harassed Noah and his sons, as for decades they built the very large boat, the ark, that God commanded.

Satan's (and society's) wisdom is a cheap substitute for God's. And faulty wisdom leads to faulty results. In his obedience, Noah was used by God to save a remnant of people, animals, and birds for a divine reboot. If he had listened to the people who came out to criticize, Noah (and all of us) would have missed out on the future God had planned.

What has God been asking you to do? What prevents your obedience?

**Remembering men of faith can only help me, God.
Your Word is filled with people who chose Your wisdom
and received a good future they had no right to demand.
Please help me to remember Your goodness.**

IT'S ALL POSSIBLE WITH GOD

And Jesus looking upon them saith, With men it is impossible, but not with God: for with God all things are possible.

MARK 10:27

One day, Jesus challenged His disciples' way of thinking. Concerning heavenly issues, He said, "Children, how hard is it for them that trust in riches to enter into the kingdom of God! It is easier for a camel to go through the eye of a needle, than for a rich man to enter into the kingdom of God" (Mark 10:24–25).

Who then can be saved? they wondered, though they dared not ask Him to further explain. But Jesus went on to teach the disciples this simple truth about salvation for anyone, rich or the poor: Without God eternal salvation is absolutely impossible. With God, though, "all things are possible."

This world presents many distractions that can keep men from truly seeking God: money, power, popularity, sex, you name it. When we consider men who seem to ignore God because they're so fully invested in fulfilling their own desires, we may simply write them off as being beyond God's reach.

But when you consider such men, remember Jesus' words: "With God, all things are possible"—and then devote yourself to prayer. Wisdom says they need to know the God who did the humanly impossible for them.

Lord Jesus, remind me to never think of anyone—no matter how far they are from You—as beyond Your reach.

THE FOOLISHNESS OF A DIVIDED HEART

Now therefore fear the L*ORD, and serve him in sincerity and in truth: and put away the gods which your fathers served on the other side of the flood, and in Egypt; and serve ye the* L*ORD.*

JOSHUA 24:14

Wisdom understands that you'll serve someone. It also knows who to serve.

This revelation calls you to follow God in obedience and do so sincerely, believing that He is truth. True wisdom doesn't consider God one of several options. It sets aside anything you may have served in the past and welcomes a close friendship with the Creator of all things.

The Israelites struggled with this idea as they finally walked away from their slavery in Egypt. They struggled to obey. They struggled to believe the truth. They struggled with putting away those things that competed against a friendship with God.

He would work, hard, on these people, spending centuries trying to remove the foolishness of a divided heart. With them, as with us, God wants to provide a new heart totally changed by His love, forgiveness, and provision.

Today, you can serve God in sincerity and truth. You can put away the idols of money, fame, sex, or power that others serve, choosing to honor and follow only the Lord. This is true wisdom.

Why is it so easy to slip back into old habits, Lord? Please use what I know about You to change my desires and pursuits. I don't want to live with the foolishness of a divided heart.

SPIRIT-FILLED LEADERSHIP

Wherefore, brethren, look ye out among you seven men of honest report, full of the Holy Ghost and wisdom, whom we may appoint over this business.
Acts 6:3

The early days of the church in Jerusalem came with challenges. As the church grew, a dispute arose regarding the fair distribution of food to widows. Since the apostles needed to focus on their primary duties of prayer and preaching the Word, they recommended that the church choose seven honest men, full of the Holy Spirit and wisdom, to oversee the business aspects of the church. They became the first deacons.

A Spirit-filled life isn't just for deacons though. Every Christian should endeavor to such an obedient way of life, since it leads to godly wisdom. That's the message of Acts 5:32, which shortly preceded this scene in chapter 6: "And we are his witnesses of these things; and so is also the Holy Ghost, whom God hath given to them that obey him." Romans 8:13 offers even more insight: "For if ye live after the flesh, ye shall die: but if ye through the Spirit do mortify the deeds of the body, ye shall live."

If your church needed the type of leaders the church in Jerusalem did (and it surely does), would it be able to call on you?

Lord, show me how to obey You today as I mortify the deeds of my body.

FOUR WISE MEN

As for these four children, God gave them knowledge and skill in all learning and wisdom: and Daniel had understanding in all visions and dreams.

DANIEL 1:17

An invasion forced many Jews to march off to Babylon as slaves. Most would never return to their homeland. Everything was new and these slaves would need to learn much to adjust to a new culture and roles.

Four young men really impressed the Babylonian officials, because they were not only smart, they were wise. Daniel, Shadrach, Meshach and Abednego were these men. God gave them their wisdom, and their difficult circumstances were informed by an understanding very different from a high IQ.

Daniel stands out because the stories of his life all point to wisdom. It included integrity, honesty, and humility. He didn't always say things people wanted to hear, but whatever Daniel said they needed to hear. The wisdom he offered greatly benefited the kingdom he served.

Our circumstances don't need to be perfect in order for us to become wise. Sometimes wisdom is discovered in hard places.

Lord God, please remind me that hard times can be very useful in my learning, understanding, and applying the things that will help me to become wise.

ABUNDANT LIFE

The thief cometh not, but for to steal, and to kill, and to destroy: I am come that they might have life, and that they might have it more abundantly.

John 10:10

What comes to mind when you hear the word *abundant*? Lots of money or possessions? Plenty of power and prestige? None of these things are bad in and of themselves; they can even be blessings from the hand of God. But when Jesus promised those who follow Him an abundant life, He wasn't talking about anything so small and unimportant.

In the New Testament, *abundant* means "exceedingly beyond measure," a quantity considerably greater than we should expect. When Jesus said He would give life "more abundantly," He was talking about what He promises to do within us. This starts at the very moment we turn to Him for salvation and continues throughout our lives, always leading to much better things both here and in heaven to come.

Our part in receiving the abundant life is to simply follow Jesus' invitation: "Abide in me, and I in you. As the branch cannot bear fruit of itself, except it abide in the vine; no more can ye, except ye abide in me" (John 15:4).

Jesus, I want the abundant life You have promised. Help me to focus not on temporal abundance but on the spiritual abundance the Bible says I have when I abide in You.

PROUD, NOT PRIDEFUL

Pride goeth before destruction, and an haughty spirit before a fall.
Proverbs 16:18

There is a difference between feeling proud and being prideful. It's okay to feel proud of your son at his Little League games. You know he's afraid of the ball, yet he showed courage by stepping up to the plate. That feeling of pleasure with your son is similar to the way God feels when we live by faith and earnestly seek Him (Hebrews 11:6).

To be prideful, though, is to exult in your own abilities or to have an outsized view of yourself. In this sense, pride is not that different from idol worship. Pride sets God aside—though He provides all human talents—and worships the gift above the giver. Anything that displaces God can rightly be thought of as an idol.

So the book of Proverbs provides a clear and simple warning: If you're prideful, you will eventually fall on your face. God does not exalt those who exalt themselves. On the other hand, Jesus, who humbled Himself to save us (Philippians 2:8), taught that consciously lowering ourselves causes God to lift us up (Luke 14:11).

Wisdom is found in humility.

Lord, forgive me for the times I've been prideful. May humility mark my life, for Your glory alone.

CHANGE YOUR CLOTHES

Wherefore seeing we also are compassed about with so great a cloud of witnesses, let us lay aside every weight, and the sin which doth so easily beset us, and let us run with patience the race that is set before us.

HEBREWS 12:1

Marathon runners prefer light clothes for a number of reasons—reduced weight, freedom of movement, body temperature regulation, even the prevention of skin irritation. And then there's the issue of aerodynamics. Tight-fitting clothes create less air resistance than loose garments, reducing the flapping that creates drag. Billowing clothes can catch the air and act like a parachute, slowing the runner down.

In today's scripture, the Greek work rendered "beset" is *euperistatos*. According to Strong's Concordance, it means "thwarting (a racer) in every direction (figuratively)." Our sin acts like loose clothes on a runner. It drags us down, keeping us from what God intends.

The good news is, we get to choose the type of clothing we wear. We don't have to run the Christian race in baggy, heavy clothes. And God gives us the wisdom to "lay aside every weight." Today, let's be sure we're not carrying a single ounce more than we need to on this long-distance run called "life."

Father, I want to run the race You've set before me with patience and endurance. Empower me to put off my sin and put on Christ.

WISE AS ROCKS

And some of the Pharisees from among the multitude said unto him, Master, rebuke thy disciples. And he answered and said unto them, I tell you that, if these should hold their peace, the stones would immediately cry out.

LUKE 19:39–40

We live in Isaiah 5:20 times. People call evil good and good evil. Darkness has become light, bitterness sweet—and vice versa. Though the world has always been colored with sin, it seems like modern culture relishes turning morality on its head.

Christians can be tempted to despair. But Jesus' words above, spoken during His "triumphal entry" into Jerusalem, should provide hope. We who live to honor God, who mourn the corruption of our human society, have an ally in creation itself.

The stones under your feet await their opportunity to cry out in praise of Jesus. The apostle Paul, noting that all creation suffered from God's curse due to Adam and Eve's sin, "also shall be delivered from the bondage of corruption into the glorious liberty of the children of God" (Romans 8:21).

Don't let the rocks and stones excel you in praise of your Lord and Savior, Jesus Christ. Speak of His greatness, loudly and often, so the inanimate objects don't have to. It can't be that tough to be wise as rocks.

Lord Jesus, You are worthy of all my praise. Thank You for creating me, keeping me, saving me, and leading me on toward heaven. You are the awesome God!

ASK GOD

If any of you lack wisdom, let him ask of God, that giveth to all men liberally, and upbraideth not; and it shall be given him.

James 1:5

The book of James was written to twelve Jewish tribes which were scattered abroad. Some believe these might be Christians who were dispersed to Judea and Samaria after the stoning of Stephen (Acts 8:1), while others believe it's a reference to believers who were driven into Assyria, Babylon, Egypt, and other kingdoms due to war. Whatever the case, their faith would be tested. James wanted them to count those moments "all joy" because the trying of faith produces patience or steadfastness. And if any of these readers lacked wisdom, they were to ask God, and it would be given to them.

What challenges are you facing today? Maybe you've been driven from your home for some reason—by a hurricane, a job loss, the breakup of your family—and you feel disillusioned. Or maybe you were displaced when your employer demanded a move from one place to another. Perhaps your crisis isn't about being dispersed—it's related to illness or finances or any number of other difficulties.

Regardless, the principle remains the same. If you lack wisdom, ask God and He will provide it.

**Lord, sometimes I just don't know what to do.
Give me the wisdom I need for my challenges.
I know that You have plenty of wisdom to offer.**

"GOD DID THAT"

I thank thee, and praise thee, O thou God of my fathers, who hast given me wisdom.
DANIEL 2:23

Daniel was considered extremely wise. He lived his life in the passionate pursuit of God's thoughts on every matter. Today's verse is part of a prayer that Daniel prayed, thanking God for giving him miraculous ways of understanding things no one else could. Good advice was in short supply—the best anyone else could do was to guess or make up stories that never actually spoke the truth. This "wisdom" caused people to make poor, dangerous choices.

Pretending you know the truth when you're only guessing is a bad approach. You risk guiding others down a dead-end street, and that doesn't help anyone.

When He answered Daniel's prayer, God revealed truths that no other human being knew. Then God gave Daniel the boldness to speak things that seemed unlikely. Yet Daniel's wisdom proved true, and his understanding brought a sense of awe to the king.

And, very wisely, Daniel was quick to acknowledge, "God did that."

I need Your wisdom, Lord. I want an understanding that's beyond any ability of my own. Help me to learn more about You and trust Your truth so I can use my wise words to praise Your name.

WHO IS THIS MAN?

He saith unto them, But whom say ye that I am? And Simon Peter answered and said, Thou art the Christ, the Son of the living God.
MATTHEW 16:15–16

You've probably heard something like this from skeptics trying to explain the identity of Jesus: He was a good, moral man and a great teacher who helped change people's lives.

Jesus was most certainly a good and moral man. He was indeed a great teacher whose words still influence people. But He was much, much more than that. He was the Son of God sent to earth to rescue hopelessly lost sinners.

Jesus once asked His disciples about the rumors of who He was. The Twelve answered that some believed Jesus was John the Baptist back from the dead, or perhaps Elijah, or Jeremiah, or one of the other prophets of old.

Jesus listened to the disciples' answers, then He dropped the question He'd intended to ask them all along, the most important question in all of human history. Who do *you* say I am?

Peter, as he so often did, spoke first: "Thou art the Christ, the Son of the living God." That was a wise response.

How would you answer someone who asked you, "Who do you think Jesus is?" It's the most important question you'll ever answer!

Heavenly Father, thank You for revealing to me who Jesus really is.

ELEVEN WISE FRIENDS

Then sent I for Eliezer, for Ariel, for Shemaiah, and for Elnathan, and for Jarib, and for Elnathan, and for Nathan, and for Zechariah, and for Meshullam, chief men; also for Joiarib, and for Elnathan, men of understanding.
EZRA 8:16

Eleven men were named. Eleven men brought their skills. Eleven men who were considered wise. This was the council. These were the trusted advisors. This was safety.

You'll make some decisions on your own. All men do. But having a core group of fellow believers who have proven wise can give you a perspective on subjects you may be unfamiliar with. This group of men doesn't show up because of a popularity poll. They don't arrive with pet theories. They simply add substance to any discussion, and if they don't have answers they say so. Then they listen carefully to others who do have insight.

Do you ever send out a call for help from other men you trust? Would you consider doing that? What value would you place on friendships that provide a greater understanding of issues you're concerned about?

God will always be the ultimate wisdom giver. But sometimes He uses wise friends.

Lord God, please lead me to friends I can trust and then help me to ask and heed their advice. I know that You often speak Your wisdom through wise friends.

TAKE HEED

Wherefore let him that thinketh he standeth take heed lest he fall.
1 CORINTHIANS 10:12

In his book *Mere Christianity*, C. S. Lewis took aim at pride. "According to Christian teachers," Lewis wrote, "the essential vice, the utmost evil, is Pride. Unchastity, anger, greed, drunkenness, and all that, are mere fleabites in comparison: it was through Pride that the devil became the devil: Pride leads to every other vice: it is the complete anti-God state of mind."

A Christian who believes he has all the answers is not only unteachable. He's basically under the false impression that he doesn't need God. Proverbs 16:18 warns against such high-mindedness: "Pride goeth before destruction, and an haughty spirit before a fall." To this end, the Christian who believes he can stand on his own probably doesn't fear falling—so he does little to protect himself from it.

The wise Christian takes heed of his sinful nature and guards himself against it via a steady diet of scripture, worship, prayer, fasting, fellowship, and accountability. As he does so, he can stand in the power of the Holy Spirit, rather than his own.

Heavenly Father, I don't want pride to derail Your work in my life. Please alert me to self-sufficiency in my thinking, and give me the wisdom and strength to banish it.

THE PERFECT KNOWLEDGE OF GOD

Such knowledge is too wonderful for me;
it is high, I cannot attain unto it.
PSALM 139:6

Biblical knowledge is good—very good. So is godly wisdom and heaven-inspired understanding. But within our faith lives, some knowledge is just beyond us. . .and this is a good thing too.

In Psalm 139, David ponders God's creative abilities and His indescribable knowledge of everything He created. The thought blew David away. He couldn't grasp how perfectly deep and comprehensive God's knowledge of us is.

God knows all the details of our daily lives, including every unspoken thought in our minds (verse 2). He is aware of every word we speak (verse 4). He guides our lives toward His preordained purposes with gentle, sovereign care (verse 5). David's response? It is all "too wonderful for me."

Like David, we should come away from these realizations with reverent awe and worship. What a joy it is to serve a God who cares and knows about every detail of our lives, even down to the number of hairs on our heads (Matthew 10:30). What amazing comfort to know that this same God, who also knows our many faults, still wants to redeem us and call us His children!

We would be wise to meditate on these things, even as they surpass our capacity to fully understand.

God, I praise You for knowing me and loving me. Help me to seek to know You better.

GROW IN GRACE

But grow in grace, and in the knowledge of our Lord and Saviour Jesus Christ.
2 PETER 3:18

Peter's final words in this letter are an admonition to grow in grace and in the knowledge of Jesus. But how do you do that? The nineteenth-century British pastor Charles Spurgeon preached a sermon on today's scripture and offers profound insight into this question.

"If you would have more faith, keep your eye on Jesus," Spurgeon said. "The wounds of Christ on Calvary are the mothers of faith; these are the breast from which faith must draw its nourishment. If you would grow in faith, you must live near to the cross. The sweet flower of faith was first sown in Christ's precious blood, and it must be watered by it every day. Know more of Christ; think more of Him; and your faith will increase."

A wise Christian understands that his life is not his own. He takes up his cross and follows Jesus—wherever the Lord leads. Believers are willing to put their own dreams and desires to death for the sake of Christ. They think more highly of others than themselves, love their enemies, and pray for all who "despitefully use" them (Matthew 5:44).

As we live out our faith in these ways, we grow in grace—and with that grace comes greater wisdom.

Lord, increase my knowledge of Christ and my desire to grow in grace as I follow You. Grant me the wisdom to walk faithfully in Your truth.

BEING HOLY

Speak unto all the congregation of the children of Israel, and say unto them, Ye shall be holy: for I the LORD your God am holy.

LEVITICUS 19:2

The book of Leviticus is primarily filled with rules the people of Israel were expected to follow. They didn't do a very good job of obeying, but it wasn't because God had been unclear.

It was wisdom for the Israelites to follow God's rules. It was wisdom for them to come back to the Lord after they'd decided to walk away from Him. This is true of us today as well.

When God told Moses that the Israelites should be holy in the same way He was holy, it surely sounded impossible. Some may have thought this meant they had to be perfect, being holy can also have another meaning. The idea of holiness can also refer to being set apart to do something important—which will be done with the God who's already doing important, remarkable things.

Being holy means you're willing to be useful to the God who has a good and wise plan—a plan that includes you.

**Here I am, Lord, trusting Your goodness and plan.
I am willing to be used in whatever way You think best.**

A POWERFUL WEAPON

Let the word of Christ dwell in you richly in all wisdom; teaching and admonishing one another in psalms and hymns and spiritual songs, singing with grace in your hearts to the Lord.
COLOSSIANS 3:16

Christians are "word people." We read and study the Word of God for daily wisdom. We recite creeds and confessions that believers have been speaking for hundreds of years. We sing old hymns that drive scriptural truths home, helping us to recall these truths during our most troubling times. And we sing spiritual songs to encourage our hearts and the hearts of those around us.

Did you know that Jesus Himself sang hymns, probably psalms set to music? After instituting the Lord's Supper, the apostle Matthew recalled, Jesus told the men He would not drink wine again until He did it with them in His Father's kingdom. "And when they had sung an hymn, they went out into the mount of Olives" (Matthew 26:30; Mark 14:25–26).

Using music to speak biblical truth to ourselves and others is one of the most powerful weapons we have. Let's be wise and use it.

Father, please help me to memorize psalms, hymns, and spiritual songs so I can teach and admonish fellow believers. Give me a teachable spirit to hear such truth from others as well.

DO IT GOD'S WAY

And David was displeased, because the Lord *had made a breach upon Uzzah: and he called the name of the place Perezuzzah to this day.*

2 Samuel 6:8

Poor Uzzah, struck dead for trying to do good.

Of course, there's more to the story than just that.

David, recently crowned king of all Israel, had made the newly conquered Jerusalem his capital. In a celebratory mood, he decided to bring the ark of the covenant to the city from its resting place several miles north. Along the way, David and his subjects "played before the Lord on all manner of instruments made of fir wood, even on harps, and on psalteries, and on timbrels, and on cornets, and on cymbals" (2 Samuel 6:5). The man after God's own heart was leading God's people in a rousing time of praise and worship. What could possibly be better?

Well, it would have helped for the ark the be transported properly. This gold-plated box, where God manifested Himself to Israel, was supposed to be carried by poles inserted through solid gold rings. When David moved it, the ark was simply set on an oxcart—and when the animals stumbled and Uzzah reached out to steady the load, tragedy followed.

Perhaps that seems extreme. But God sets the rules, and we are wise to follow them exactly. Don't ever do your own thing and assume God will bless you. Do everything *His* way.

Lord, thanks for Your grace—but help me to honor You by following Your rules precisely.

FOOLISH QUESTIONS

But avoid foolish questions, and genealogies, and contentions, and strivings about the law; for they are unprofitable and vain.
Titus 3:9

Titus was a Gentile, converted to Christianity under the ministry of Paul. The great apostle wanted Titus to avoid "foolish questions, genealogies, and contentions, and strivings about the law." He probably said this because, at the time, Jews often debated frivolous questions. They trusted their heritage as God's chosen people to give them authority over such matters, but Paul aptly pointed out that such discussions were unprofitable and vain for the Christian.

"There are hundreds of questions, which are thought by some people to be very important, but which have no practical bearing whatever, either upon the glory of God, or upon the holiness of man," Charles Spurgeon wrote in his commentary about this verse. "We are not to go into these matters; let those who have time to waste take up these questions."

This invites the question—what sort of foolish questions, genealogies, contentions, and strivings about the law does the modern church engage in? Which ones do you engage in? It would be wise to pray through anything that comes to mind. . .then push it aside.

Lord, search my heart today for any foolish questions and contentions. Rather than arguing over such things, may I pray for the souls of the people You've placed around me.

THOSE WHO STEP INTO THE GAP

David went down, and his servants with him, and fought against the Philistines: and David waxed faint.
2 Samuel 21:15

Israel's most famous king, David, went to battle against the Philistines. He might have remembered that his very first wartime engagement was with the Philistines. David had taken on their champion, Goliath, and won. But this was a new war—and this time David was worn out. He was approached by another giant man. . .and this time things didn't look good for the aging king.

Then one of David's warriors, Abishai, stepped into the gap between the king and the enemy Ishbibenob. Abishai did what David couldn't—he vanquished the Philistine. The soldiers all agreed that it was time for the king to stay home while the soldiers fought Israel's battles.

Wisdom sometimes means paying attention to our own physical limitations and accepting help when it's needed. God can provide the strength to do what you can't do on your own. But sometimes He may send someone to assist you. Don't foolishly reject such help.

It's easy to think I need to do everything myself, Lord. Help me to accept Your help and the help You bring my way. May I be wise enough to recognize when I need someone's aid.

WISE UNTO SALVATION

And that from a child thou hast known the holy scriptures, which are able to make thee wise unto salvation through faith which is in Christ Jesus.
2 TIMOTHY 3:15

Paul's message to Timothy in this chapter is one of grave seriousness. In the last days, perilous times will come. Men will be lovers of self, covetous, boasters, proud, blasphemers, unthankful, unholy, and despisers of those that are good. In fact, Paul promises that "all that will live godly in Christ Jesus shall suffer persecution" (2 Timothy 3:12).

How do you stand up in such times? Today's verse gives us the answer. Timothy was raised in the faith by his grandmother Lois and mother Eunice, and Paul was convinced that saving faith was now present in Timothy (2 Timothy 1:5). They had taught him the scriptures as a child, making Timothy "wise unto salvation."

Maybe that was your experience too—a faithful parent or grandparent taught you the scriptures when you were young. Or maybe you are a first-generation Christian who has been discipled by a faithful, older man. Either way, your pathway to wisdom can be found in the scriptures. Continue to feed on them and look for men who need help understanding them so they too may be wise unto salvation.

Lord, remind me to make the Bible my priority today and every day. And help me to connect with other guys who are hungry for the Word but may need help in understanding it.

BRAINPOWER AND MORE

Go to the ant, thou sluggard; consider her ways, and be wise: Which having no guide, overseer, or ruler, provideth her meat in the summer, and gathereth her food in the harvest.
Proverbs 6:6–8

This is scripture's famed passage on laziness. But it also offers encouragement for those times we feel lost and confused.

How big can an ant's brain be? And yet the little guy knows exactly what to do, when. God has made the ant wise enough to work hard now to prepare for his future time of need.

Our lives are certainly more complicated than an ant's, but we also have vastly more brainpower. . .and a direct connection to our Creator, who made us in His own image. When we're struggling, we can ask Him for wisdom (James 1:5). We've been taught by Jesus Himself to ask His Father for "our daily bread" (Matthew 6:11). We know that God cares for the birds, and that we as human beings are much more valuable to Him (Matthew 6:26; Luke 12:24).

So, if you're a lazybones, take a lesson from the ants. And if you ever feel overwhelmed by life, do the same. Those tiny creatures do what God created them to do, and they succeed. So can we. It's all a matter of prayer and obedience.

Lord God, thank You for giving me a strong mind—may I always direct it toward Your ultimate wisdom.

MEN OF PRAYER

And when he had sent them away,
[Jesus] departed into a mountain to pray.
Mark 6:46

As Christian men, it's wise for us to develop a strong, growing prayer life. Every godly man in the Old and New Testament prayed. So do godly men today.

The Gospels include several accounts of Jesus praying to His Father. He prayed at His baptism (Luke 3:21), before choosing His twelve disciples (Luke 6:12), before Peter's confession (Luke 9:18), at His transfiguration (Luke 9:29), and before He was arrested and crucified (John 17).

Jesus was the Son of God who had the power and authority to do everything His Father had sent Him to do. Yet He prayed.

Jesus was fully God and fully human. He needed to sleep, eat, breathe, and drink water—just like any of us. But to keep Himself focused and empowered to do the things He came to earth to do, He needed help from His Father in heaven. That means He needed to take regular time to connect with God through prayer.

When Jesus prayed, He set an example of consistent, regular prayer for each of us. If Jesus, the Son of God, needed to pray, how could we not follow His example?

Lord God, may I never neglect taking time to connect my heart to Yours through prayer.

KISS THE SON

Serve the Lord *with fear, and rejoice with trembling. Kiss the Son, lest he be angry, and ye perish from the way, when his wrath is kindled but a little. Blessed are all they that put their trust in him.*

Psalm 2:11–12

Since the fall of humanity, there has never been a kingdom on earth free from rebellion and strife. Human utopias don't exist. There are always existential conflicts and uprisings from within and without. A wise ruler, then, governs with both mercy and justice, treating his subjects fairly while punishing evil.

Psalm 2 serves as a royal warning from the King of the universe, whose subjects are rebelling against Him and His Son, the heir. In His mercy and grace, the King admonishes His rebellious people, giving them a chance to turn from their spiritual anarchy before He unleashes terrible and just judgment. It is utter folly for finite creatures to fight against the infinite Creator. Rather, we must "kiss the Son," paying homage to the King's appointed Ruler.

Bow to God in worshipful, reverent fear as your Lord. Praise and rejoice in His Son, Jesus, as your Savior. All who do not will perish. But those who wisely recognize and welcome God's rule in their lives will be blessed.

God, I worship You as King and praise Your Son as my Savior.

SOBER AND VIGILANT

Be sober, be vigilant; because your adversary the devil, as a roaring lion, walketh about, seeking whom he may devour.
1 PETER 5:8

The wise Christian is "sober" and "vigilant," knowing the devil is seeking ways to destroy him. *Sober* here refers to being perceptive or heedful of potential consequences. And *vigilant* indicates being watchful and staying awake, or more specifically, being continuously attentive. Put all of these ideas together and you have a clear picture: The Christian is supposed to be suspicious of danger from Satan.

Why must we be on guard to such a degree? Because Satan is coming for you. You don't have to fear him stealing your salvation, but you can be sure he wants to derail your Christian life and your effectiveness for the kingdom. He'd love to blow up your relationships, your ministry, your job. . .anything that reflects on your relationship with Jesus.

Satan knows your weaknesses, and he will try to exploit them. If you want to thwart his plans, it's wise to address your trouble spots. Seek accountability and godly counsel for them. Don't live in isolation. Surround yourself with other Christians who are seeking to stay on the narrow road, then walk arm in arm with them toward the celestial city.

Lord, as I consider my weaknesses today, I will seek out other Christians who can help me to stay sober and vigilant.

STRANGERS IN THE WATER

Drink waters out of thine own cistern, and running waters out of thine own well. . . . Let them be only thine own, and not strangers' with thee. Let thy fountain be blessed: and rejoice with the wife of thy youth.

PROVERBS 5:15, 17–18

Some people think God doesn't like sex. But that's not true! In fact, He designed the best possible context for *great* sex: marriage (Genesis 2:23–25). Numerous passages in Proverbs, the Song of Songs, and elsewhere in scripture encourage a thriving sexual relationship with your spouse. There's no other way to say it: God wants you and your wife to enjoy great sex together.

In Proverbs 5:15–23, "running waters" is a metaphor for sexual energy. The message is clear: Keep "strangers" out of the "waters" that you and your wife enjoy. Unfortunately, it can be tempting to invite a stranger to dip their toes into your waters. Pornography, flirtatious relationships, emotional affairs, secret profiles online. . .all of them are sinful and unwise. They redirect sexual energy toward someone else.

What is God's wisdom in the face of such temptations? Save all your sexual energy for your wife alone. Wisdom often requires work (Proverbs 2:1–5). So do the work necessary to keep strangers out (Matthew 5:27–30) and foster a healthy sexual relationship with your own wife.

Lord, I want to honor You in all things, even sex. Help me to invest all my energy into my marriage.

WISE LISTENING

Wherefore, my beloved brethren, let every man be swift to hear, slow to speak, slow to wrath.

James 1:19

More than forty years ago, *Discipleship Journal* published an enduring article entitled "How to Become a Good Listener." In it, author Janet Dunn wrote, "Unfortunately, many of us are too preoccupied with ourselves when we listen. Instead of concentrating on what is being said, we are busy either deciding what to say in response or mentally rejecting the other person's point of view."

In today's scripture, James instructs believers to be "swift to hear, slow to speak, slow to wrath." Part of wise hearing involves putting aside the points you want to make so you can take in what a more mature believer may be trying to communicate. That's not to say you can't ultimately disagree with him, but hear him out. Consider his words. Ask the Lord if what the man is saying is right. Ask follow-up questions for the sake of clarity. Don't fear silence. The Lord often works in the quiet places of our hearts.

Here's another benefit of wise listening: The man who is swift to hear and slow to speak won't be quick to wrath.

Lord, give me ears to hear truth and a tongue that is slow to speak. I want to become a wise listener.

TELLING THE NEXT GENERATION

We will not hide them from their children, shewing to the generation to come the praises of the Lord, *and his strength, and his wonderful works that he hath done.*
Psalm 78:4

In Isaiah 55:11, God said that His life-changing Word "shall not return unto me void, but it shall accomplish that which I please." Being all-powerful and perfectly wise, God could spread His message of salvation to the world in a myriad of ways. But in His sovereignty and lovingkindness, He chooses to spread the gospel. . .through us.

This is remarkable. Despite our sin and shortcomings, God invites us to be part of His plan to reach every people group in every corner of the world with the glorious news of salvation through faith in Jesus Christ.

And it starts with the younger generation, our own children, if we have them, and other kids we know and interact with. Are you teaching them to know and love the Lord? God has always been concerned for the generations—and He calls us to train up the younger ones.

Want to be wise in your walk with the Lord? Proclaim His greatness to children—yours and others. Herald His goodness, love, mercy, and forgiveness to adolescents. Declare His salvation through Christ to the next generation.

Lord, thank You for involving me in Your plan of salvation. Help me tell the next generation of the wonderful works You've done.

NEW CREATION WISDOM

All scripture is given by inspiration of God, and is profitable for doctrine, for reproof, for correction, for instruction in righteousness: that the man of God may be perfect, thoroughly furnished unto all good works.
2 Timothy 3:16–17

Some words you can read will help you make good choices, reject bad opinions, and follow a great God. But those words aren't found in many places. The truth is that many of us have looked for them. Maybe we were curious to compare what God said with what others believe. Maybe we were seeking a belief system with better terms and options. Stop looking! Only God and His Word offer life.

The words He inspired are perfectly aligned to correct our thinking, redirect our actions, and instruct us in the ways of right living. It is a mark of wisdom to accept this, believe it, and allow it to change everything about you.

This means that God can transform you into what He calls a new creation. He doesn't give a list of traits that are necessary to merit His help. He isn't picky about candidates for belief. He accepts all who come to Him by saying, "read My word, learn from Me, and discover real wisdom."

What I read is what You've said, Lord. What I follow should be the directions You've given. Please give me the wisdom to read, follow, and believe.

ESSENTIAL RELATIONSHIPS

Moses hands were heavy; and they took a stone, and put it under him, and he sat thereon; and Aaron and Hur stayed up his hands, the one on the one side, and the other on the other side; and his hands were steady until the going down of the sun.

EXODUS 17:12

Behold the wisdom of relationship. It was on full display in Exodus 17. God told Moses that in a certain battle His people would prevail when Moses held up his hands. But when Moses lowered his hands, the Israelites would be overcome by the enemy. That sounds easy enough, right? Anyone can hold up his hands! But that becomes harder and harder the longer you keep your arms stretched out. Every new moment becomes agony.

When Moses rested the people were overpowered. The wisdom of Exodus 17:12 is that the hardest things can be much easier with help. God helped by keeping a promise; Aaron and Hur helped because, as friends, they stepped up to assist Moses in doing what he struggled to do alone.

Friendships aren't just a nice idea—they are essential to our well-being.

You're the perfect example of a friend, Father. Help me to rely on You and then on friends who also rely on You. Wisdom is found in working together with You.

LIKE A BEREAN

And the brethren immediately sent away Paul and Silas by night unto Berea: who coming thither went into the synagogue of the Jews. These were more noble than those in Thessalonica, in that they received the word with all readiness of mind, and searched the scriptures daily, whether those things were so.

Acts 17:10–11

In a Pew Research Center study, more than half (55 percent) of the Christians surveyed said they read the Bible once or twice a month, several times a year, seldom or never, or didn't know. Only 45 percent of respondents said they read scripture once a week or more often. This would indicate that more than half are willing to listen to the Word being preached, but they're not actually examining it for themselves during the week. It's difficult to exhibit biblical wisdom without searching the scriptures daily, as the Berean Christians were commended for doing so in today's passage.

How often do you search the scriptures? Do you believe your ears are spiritually tuned to the truth? Can you detect error from a Christian leader when you hear it?

Wisdom, obviously, is in knowing God deeply through a careful study of His Word. Why not commit today to being "more noble" like the believers of Berea?

Lord God, I know that if I want to be wise, I have to search the scriptures daily. Give me the insight I need to know that what I'm hearing from other Christians is accurate.

JUDGMENT

Thus speaketh the LORD of hosts, saying, Execute true judgment, and shew mercy and compassions every man to his brother: and oppress not the widow, nor the fatherless, the stranger, nor the poor; and let none of you imagine evil against his brother in your heart.

ZECHARIAH 7:9–10

We often think the idea of judgment hinges on punishment for wrongdoing. But Zechariah 7 seems to suggest that it's also about helping people who've been poorly treated and oppressed. This judgment doesn't resemble revenge or other forms of payback—it involves mercy, compassion, and a personal refusal to hold people down. This list is filled with ideas on how you can help.

The concept is less about making sure someone gets what's coming to them than ensuring that those who are oppressed get the help they need. It's also a reminder that you should never be the one to take advantage of the widow, the orphan, the stranger, or the economically disadvantaged.

Feel free to add these ideas to your own priority list. These are things God wants from those who follow Him. And it's always wise to pay attention to that which means something to God.

Sometimes I think Your justice is all about punishing wrongdoing, Lord. Thank You for the reminder that there are times when justice is best served by Your kindness.

UNSEEN THINGS

While we look not at the things which are seen, but at the things which are not seen: for the things which are seen are temporal; but the things which are not seen are eternal.
2 Corinthians 4:18

We can spend the majority of our lives on things we see. We invest time and money in our own physical appearance, or our homes, or our cars, or the vacations and other pleasures this world offers. But the problem is, all these things are passing away. They are only temporal. Do you really want to get to the end of your life and realize you spent more of it on things that don't really matter?

"Surely the men who make this world to be their highest joy find at the last it biteth like a serpent and stingeth as an adder," said Charles Spurgeon in a sermon based on today's text. "They indulge their passions to the destruction of their souls. Do not, therefore, mark carnal joy as specially to be desired. But are we never to have anything special to mark? Oh yes; carefully mark down the eternal things. Did the Lord appear to you? Mark that down. Did you win a soul to Christ? Mark that down. Did you have sweet answers to prayer? Mark that down. Those are things of special note."

Lord, set my eyes today and every day on unseen things—things that will matter for all eternity.

FACELIFT

A man's wisdom maketh his face to shine,
and the boldness of his face shall be changed.
ECCLESIASTES 8:1

One great benefit of wisdom is the change it makes in your appearance. That may sound strange...it doesn't seem as if wisdom is anything like cosmetic surgery. But what if it actually is? What if wisdom changes us internally to such a degree that it's noticeable on the outside?

Fear leaves lines of concern etched on a face. Anger draws new features that intimidate others. Bitterness carves unintended storylines around lips that speak unpleasantly.

Wisdom, though, dismisses those negative thought patterns that constantly work to reform your face and deform your heart.

While wisdom can't remove the wrinkles of time, it can and will make your face to shine. It will bring a healthy and holy boldness to you, something that other people will notice. And maybe they'll be moved to ask what makes you so different.

Then you can wisely and winsomely explain.

Heavenly Father, please guide my choices so that my face reflects the beautiful heart of the wise.

GUARDING YOUR MIND

Ye have heard that it was said by them of old time,
Thou shalt not commit adultery: but I say unto you,
That whosoever looketh on a woman to lust after her hath
committed adultery with her already in his heart.
MATTHEW 5:27–28

In this scripture passage, Jesus quotes God's seventh commandment—"Thou shalt not commit adultery" (Exodus 20:14)—and expands on its true meaning. He points out that sexual impurity is about more than just "the act."

In Old Testament times, God had forbidden any sexual activity outside of marriage, and that commandment still stands today. But Jesus taught that the issue isn't just where we take our bodies—it also includes where we allow our hearts and minds to go.

Long ago, Job was on to something when he said, "I made a covenant with mine eyes; why then should I think upon a maid?" (Job 31:1). In other Bible translations, the interpretation of Job's words is that he made sure his eyes didn't lead his mind toward impure thinking. That's some excellent wisdom!

In today's sex-saturated world, avoiding images that cause lust is no easy task. For us as Christian men today, it's a matter of commitment... to our wives, to our families, and to our Lord.

Dear Jesus, help me to keep my heart pure from impure thinking by making sure my eyes avoid anything that could cause me to lust.

PROPER PERSPECTIVE

What is man, that thou art mindful of him? and the son of man, that thou visitest him?
PSALM 8:4

We are quite good at thinking of ourselves. In fact, we're epically good at that.

From the moment we're born, we are hyper-self-focused. When we don't get what we want, we fuss, cry, and pitch a fit. (Babies do too.) As we get older, we begin to build our own little fiefdoms, trying to amass and assert power, prestige, and sway in whatever circles of influence we travel. We so easily become the center of our own little universe.

Then we read Psalm 8, a much-needed wake-up call. This beautiful psalm was written by David, who was God's anointed king, the most important man among millions in Israel. But when David—perhaps strolling along the terrace of his palace in Jerusalem—looked into the heavens one night, he was stunned. Considering the vastness of God's creation, he realized how small he truly was. That realization comes down through history as Psalm 8:4.

Our universe is indescribably immense, and the God who created and governs it is far greater. In comparison, we are laughably small. And yet, God loves each one of us deeply, to the point of giving up His own Son to bring us into fellowship with Him.

We are wise to ponder such things.

Who am I, Lord, that You are mindful of me? Yet You are, and I'm so thankful.

MORTIFIED FLESH

Love not the world, neither the things that are in the world. If any man love the world, the love of the Father is not in him.

1 JOHN 2:15

You might come across a verse like this and wonder what it means in relation to John 3:16, which says, "God so loved the world." How can God love the world while the individual Christian isn't supposed to?

According to *Baker's Evangelical Dictionary of Biblical Theology*, "The biblical concept of world falls into five categories: the physical world, the human world, the moral world, the temporal world, and the coming world." While the same Greek word is used in John 3:16 as the apostle used in today's verse, they mean different things.

The Christian is to love humanity, while rejecting the world system (referred to as the moral world—people who are indifferent or hostile to God). The next verse (1 John 2:16) defines what John is warning against: "For all that is in the world, the lust of the flesh, and the lust of the eyes, and the pride of life, is not of the Father, but is of the world."

What are you currently doing to put to death the lust of your flesh and eyes, the pride of your life? Romans 8:13 calls this mortifying the flesh, and it takes work—but work that is empowered by God through your willing spirit.

Lord, I reject this sinful world system. Please help me to mortify my flesh today.

GOD'S ATTENTION BRINGS PEACE

The Lord lift up his countenance upon thee, and give thee peace.
Numbers 6:26

You have God's attention. If you don't believe this then consider a prayer from one of the very earliest books in the Bible. God told Moses to speak life-giving words over the people of Israel. This blessing was for those who'd left Egypt but lived with the fear of what they didn't know. They stressed over less-than-ideal conditions. They refused to consider the promises God gave them for a future home that would exceed anything they'd yet experienced.

These strugglers were blessed with the words of the scripture above. Moses prayed for God to pay attention to the Israelites, and for Him to give them His peace.

You probably need this blessing for yourself. You need to know that God can (and does) pay attention to you, that He wants to bring peace into your circumstances—the ones you face today and the ones that will eventually show up.

Wisdom recognizes this blessing and takes it to heart. It's always easier to experience the goodness of God when you're convinced that it does exist.

I want to be blessed in this way, God—to believe that You're paying attention and that You're ready and willing to give me peace. Please help me to receive Your goodness.

SOW RIGHTEOUSNESS

Be not deceived; God is not mocked:
for whatsoever a man soweth, that shall he also reap.
GALATIANS 6:7

You cannot plant a field with potatoes and expect carrots to grow. Nor would you want that. Farmers and gardeners plant what they expect to grow. It only makes sense.

In the spiritual realm, we can't plant sin and expect a beautiful crop of righteousness to appear. Sowing sin is actually considered a mockery of God. It's like saying He'll never notice—that our behavior doesn't matter to Him. Today's verse warns against such foolishness.

If you want righteousness to grow, you must plant it—after pulling up sin by its roots. Bible reading and study, a devoted prayer life, consistent Christian fellowship, regular corporate worship, serving the Lord in various ministries, reading good Christian books, private time with God. . .all are ways to plant righteousness.

As you do these things, you'll begin to notice small shoots of wisdom and goodness appearing in your life—which is the work of God Himself. You do the planting, and He'll grant the increase (1 Corinthians 3:6).

Lord, please help me to pull up the roots of sin in my life so there will be fertile ground to sow and reap righteousness.

MAKE WAY

Then Jonathan and David made a covenant, because he loved him as his own soul. And Jonathan stripped himself of the robe that was upon him, and gave it to David, and his garments, even to his sword, and to his bow, and to his girdle.

1 Samuel 18:3–4

Jonathan should have become the second king of Israel. His father, Saul, was the man God chose in response to the people's demand for a human ruler. Sadly, Saul's selfishness and folly caused God to declare an end to his royal house (1 Samuel 15). But he would remain on the throne for several years while God raised David from the obscurity of watching his father's sheep.

When David defeated the Philistine giant Goliath, Jonathan quickly recognized the young man's qualities and "the soul of Jonathan was knit with the soul of David" (1 Samuel 18:1). Today's scripture, describing the handing over of royal clothing and military equipment, indicates Jonathan realized David was destined for leadership. Jonathan would protect his beloved friend against his own father's murderous intentions, and suffer Saul's emotional abuse for doing so (see 1 Samuel 20:30–31).

What about us? Can we admit that others may surpass us in wisdom and ability, and make way for them to accomplish their God-given objectives? It's always better to support God's plan than resist it—to quote a thoughtful Pharisee from a millennium later, "lest haply ye be found even to fight against God" (Acts 5:39).

Lord, keep me humble and ready to serve at whatever level You choose.

TEST ALL THINGS

Prove all things; hold fast that which is good.
Abstain from all appearance of evil.
1 THESSALONIANS 5:21–22

Some translations use the word *test* instead of *prove* in these verses. The idea is this: Don't automatically believe everything you hear about God or the Bible just because someone you know said it.

Bible commentator Albert Barnes described what this passage means to Christians: "In the various opinions and doctrines which were submitted to them for adoption, they were to apply the appropriate tests from reason and the word of God, and what they found to be true they were to embrace; what was false they were to reject. Christianity does not require people to disregard their reason, or to be credulous. It does not expect them to believe anything because others say it is so."

Test everything that anyone says about God or His Word, whether it comes from your pastor, Sunday school teacher, small group leader, best friend, mentor, or favorite radio preacher. It's not that you assume they're ignorant or deceitful. . .but every human being is fallible. Wisdom demands that we base all of our beliefs on the inerrant, unchanging Word of God.

Father, help me to test everything I hear about You and Your Word. I don't want to be suspicious of other Christians, just diligent.

ON DISPLAY

O God, thou knowest my foolishness; and my sins are not hid from thee.
Psalm 69:5

All the world's a stage,
And all the men and women merely players;
They have their exits and their entrances;
And one man in his time plays many parts,
His acts being seven ages.

These words of William Shakespeare, from his play *As You Like It*, ring with poignant truth. But while much of our lives are on display for others to see, no one knows everything about us. And that's a good thing—if all of our faults and foibles, shortcomings, unkind words, selfishness, self-righteousness, and hateful thoughts were on full display, who would want to be around us? Would anyone love us?

God knows all of these things. He sees everything we do, hears every word we say, and knows every thought we entertain. Our lives, from end to end, are on display for Him. And yet He is not repulsed. Instead, He reaches out to us with open arms of love. He moved heaven and earth to offer the salvation we so desperately needed.

The wise man humbly ponders this. And rather than shrinking back in shame, he runs into the embrace of His Savior, who gladly receives all through faith.

God, thank You for loving me despite all my sins and shortcomings. I am grateful that Jesus makes me righteous and whole.

BUILDING UPON THE ROCK

Therefore whosoever heareth these sayings of mine, and doeth them, I will liken him unto a wise man, which built his house upon a rock: and the rain descended, and the floods came, and the winds blew, and beat upon that house; and it fell not: for it was founded upon a rock.

MATTHEW 7:24–25

You don't need to be a master architect or a longtime homebuilder to know that if a house is to stand in the face of storms and flooding, it must be built on a strong, immovable foundation. Without that? Well, you'd better have a very generous homeowners insurance policy.

Jesus closed His Sermon on the Mount with words that encourage and challenge His followers to build their lives on His teaching—and by extension on Jesus Himself.

If you want to experience a lasting, unshakable Christian life, you'd be wise to build your faith on the equally unshakable foundation of God's Word. A life with a weak foundation will be a life filled with frustration and defeat. But the Word of God provides the solid grounding you need to weather any imaginable storm.

Lord Jesus, thank You for being my rock and my foundation. May I build a solid, lasting faith life on the sure foundation of Your Word.

LISTEN UP

Turn you at my reproof: behold, I will pour out my spirit unto you, I will make known my words unto you.

PROVERBS 1:23

Though the words above sound like God's, they are actually attributed to "Wisdom" (Proverbs 1:20). Personified as a woman, "She crieth in the chief place of concourse, in the openings of the gates: in the city she uttereth her words, saying, How long, ye simple ones, will ye love simplicity? and the scorners delight in their scorning, and fools hate knowledge?" (verses 21–22).

Of course, Wisdom originates with God, so whatever "she" tells us will be what He would say. And in today's scripture, Wisdom implores, "Turn you at my reproof."

Reproof is an expression of strong disapproval. Haven't we all heard that at some time, from a friend, pastor, wife—or within our own spirit? Not every negative voice should be heeded, but God will often send Wisdom to turn us from some foolish path. If the voice you're hearing confirms what you know God's Word says, listen up.

When we stop to consider Wisdom's call, she then pours out her spirit and makes her words known. All of this is true of Wisdom's source too.

When you hear Wisdom's reproof, stop. Change direction. There's a reward for listening but trouble for plowing ahead (see the nine verses following today's scripture).

I don't want to be a fool, Lord. Tune my ear to Wisdom's call, and strengthen me to obey.

DO THE NEXT THING

But be ye doers of the word, and not hearers only, deceiving your own selves.
JAMES 1:22

A new Christian was struggling with some deep theological concepts. He finally decided to approach his Sunday school teacher for clarification. The teacher invited the man to his home where the new believer explained his desire for understanding. The teacher listened patiently, then asked the man if he had been baptized yet. The answer was no.

"Then do the thing you know to do first," the teacher replied.

As you encounter clear teachings in the Bible, be quick to obey them. Being "doers of the word" is an outward indicator of what's going on inside our hearts. So is the act of *not* obeying.

When we aren't doers of the word, we deceive ourselves, no matter what sophisticated arguments we may try to make. Don't attempt to reason your way through the Christian life. Obedience to what you know to be true will lead to greater wisdom and insight.

Lord, may it never be said about me that I'm a hearer of the Word but not a doer. Show me the truth and help me to obey it.

HOW TO ANSWER A FOOL

Answer not a fool according to his folly, lest thou also be like unto him. Answer a fool according to his folly, lest he be wise in his own conceit.
PROVERBS 26:4–5

Some people struggle to believe that the Bible can be trusted. They point to verses like these and claim God's Word contradicts itself. But these verses don't reveal an error in scripture—they unveil a great truth: God provides wisdom for each scenario you will encounter.

The book of Proverbs doesn't provide pat answers to easy questions. It provides wisdom. And the truly wise will know what to say—or not say—and when.

Proverbs is like the menu on a streaming service offering a thousand short videos. Each one you click on reveals God's design for daily life. Each verse gives insight into God's heart, revealing what He values. Proverbs is not a book of individual promises—it's a collection of wise sayings that describe how life happens most of the time.

Today's verses demonstrate that the same answer doesn't apply to every situation. Life, like God, is complex. Living wisely includes both speaking up and remaining silent. And we can always request God's wisdom for each circumstance (James 1:5).

Lord, please help me to know when it is time to speak up and when it is time to remain silent.

LISTEN TO JESUS

The officers answered, Never man spake like this man. Then answered them the Pharisees, Are ye also deceived? Have any of the rulers or of the Pharisees believed on him?
JOHN 7:46–48

Jesus' appearance at the feast of tabernacles highlights the diverging opinions about Him. As He taught in the temple, people both murmured and marveled. Some said He was demon possessed (John 7:20), while others believed, asking, "When Christ cometh, will he do more miracles than these?" (verse 31).

The chief priests and Pharisees, leaders who felt threatened by Jesus, decided to send men to arrest Him. When the officers returned empty-handed, saying, "Never man spake like this man," the leadership was incensed. "Are ye also deceived?" they mocked. "Have any of the rulers or of the Pharisees believed on him?"

In reality, the officers were the wise ones. Having heard Jesus directly, they made their own judgment based on His words. It didn't matter to them what the "intelligent class" thought.

Today, many oppose and mock Jesus. Others claim His name while contradicting His teaching. As Christians, we must listen to *Him*, ordering our lives by scripture, regardless of anyone else's view. Let's even double-check our favorite teachers, as the noble Bereans did with the apostle Paul: "They received the word with all readiness of mind, and searched the scriptures daily, whether those things were so" (Acts 17:11).

Lord, help me tune out this world's opinions to focus entirely on You.

NOT KEEPING IT SIMPLE

The law of the LORD is perfect, converting the soul:
the testimony of the LORD is sure, making wise the simple.
PSALM 19:7

We love when life is simple: A simple day at work? Nice! A simple commute to work? Hopefully! A simple tax return? May it be so! A simple recipe for dinner? Much needed! A simple conversation with our wife before bedtime? Please!

But when the Bible talks about being simple, it's usually not a good thing. Scripture often uses *simple* as a synonym for spiritual foolishness and hard-heartedness.

Psalm 19:7 tells us that "the testimony of the LORD is sure, making wise the simple." Because God's Word is true for all of life, it holds the key to knowledge, wisdom, and salvation. Because the law of the Lord is perfect, we can trust that it contains the truth that converts our souls.

Do spiritually simple people suddenly have an epiphany of their own accord to understand their great need for biblical wisdom and God's saving grace? No, only the Spirit of God can enlighten darkened souls. When God graciously awakens our hearts and minds to the saving truth of the gospel, we must respond with repentance and faith. Then, He will grow a continuing love in our hearts for the truth of scripture, making us wise indeed.

Lord, please make me wise through Your perfect Word.

SWEET SAVOUR OF CHRIST

Let no corrupt communication proceed out of your mouth, but that which is good to the use of edifying, that it may minister grace unto the hearers.
Ephesians 4:29

Have you gone into the kitchen and discovered a foul odor? And then you saw it, some leftover, long-forgotten piece of food, rotting. You couldn't toss it in the trash quickly enough. That food was not only of no use to you or your family now, it had become an active nuisance—a hindrance to your well-being.

The Greek word rendered "corrupt" in today's scripture means rotten or worthless. Rotten words are not edifying. In fact, they are a hindrance to edification. You've been around believers who have spewed rotten words, and you couldn't escape from their presence fast enough. Most likely, you've even spouted rotten words yourself. Next time you feel that nasty stuff rising up inside you, toss it into the trash. Then spray the world's greatest air freshener, the "sweet savour of Christ" (2 Corinthians 2:15).

Father, may I only minister grace unto the hearers of my words today.

DON'T BARGAIN, TRUST

And Jephthah vowed a vow unto the Lord, *and said, If thou shalt without fail deliver the children of Ammon into mine hands, then it shall be, that whatsoever cometh forth of the doors of my house to meet me, when I return in peace from the children of Ammon, shall surely be the* Lord's, *and I will offer it up for a burnt offering.*

Judges 11:30–31

Jephthah's vow has been described as "rash" or "tragic." And why not? This judge of Israel asked God for victory in battle, promising that afterward he would sacrifice whatever stepped out of his house. Was he expecting a goat or chicken? It was, in fact, his only child.

The story warns against foolish promises. But there was a deeper issue for Jephthah, one that we as Christian men today do well to consider: When God has called and empowered a person for service, that's enough. No embellishment is necessary or desirable.

Jephthah had dealt wisely with the king of Ammon, denying his demand for Israelite land. "Wilt not thou possess that which Chemosh thy god giveth thee to possess? So whomsoever the Lord our God shall drive out from before us, them will we possess" (Judges 11:24). When the Ammonite king ignored the message, "the Spirit of the Lord came upon Jephthah" (verse 29). Heading to battle in this power, though, Jephthah seemed to hesitate, making the foolish vow in today's scripture.

Let's not make a similar mistake. With God's promises and presence, we need nothing more. Our trust honors Him more than any promised sacrifice ever could.

Lord, I trust You. That's enough.

FAITH AS A MUSTARD SEED

And Jesus said unto them, Because of your unbelief: for verily I say unto you, If ye have faith as a grain of mustard seed, ye shall say unto this mountain, Remove hence to yonder place; and it shall remove; and nothing shall be impossible unto you.

MATTHEW 17:20

The incredible privilege of Jesus' disciples—the opportunity to experience His wisdom, love, and power in person every day—didn't guarantee their success in every endeavor. One time, the Lord found that they had tried but failed, miserably, to cast a stubborn evil spirit out of a boy.

After healing the boy Himself, Jesus addressed the obvious question: Why couldn't the disciples cast out this demon?

Jesus spoke very plainly. The cause of the disciples' failure that day was a lack of faith. All they needed to accomplish anything, He said, was faith the size of a mustard seed. That's only a tiny fraction of an inch in diameter.

Jesus' lesson for the disciples applies to all of us today. When you place your faith—even if it's very small—in a mighty God who can do anything, you have done wisely. And nothing will be impossible for you.

Jesus, help me to remember it's not the size of my faith that matters. It's that I put my faith in You! Please accomplish powerful things through me.

BEHAVING WISELY

When Saul saw that he behaved himself very wisely, he was afraid of him.
1 SAMUEL 18:15

King Saul didn't expect the young man, David, to defeat the Philistine champion, Goliath. Saul didn't expect David to continue to be a valiant warrior. Saul didn't expect this young man to be chosen as king by the prophet Samuel. But all of these things happened.

When Saul witnessed David's strength, commitment, and wise decision-making, the first king of Israel became afraid of the young man. Though Saul had no evidence of a developing coup, he chose to view David as an enemy. And that was in spite of the fact that David had helped the king win many battles.

Foolish people are intimidated by wisdom—they're afraid of wise people. Foolish people fear that everything they've worked for will be taken by someone who's more popular. Foolish people don't talk to God about their fears. . .they just keep digging deeper holes for themselves.

Since he had "behaved himself very wisely," David positioned himself for God's blessing. By behaving wisely, we'll receive God's goodness as well.

Lord God, please help me to behave myself very wisely, so I can position myself for Your blessing. I don't ever want to be like King Saul.

FLEEING LUSTS

Flee also youthful lusts: but follow righteousness, faith, charity, peace, with them that call on the Lord out of a pure heart.
2 TIMOTHY 2:22

Today's passage was written to the apostle Paul's charge, Timothy. He wanted this young minister of the gospel to flee "youthful lusts." This would certainly include sensual desires but also common passions such as pride, ambition, and a hunger for power.

Then Paul gave Timothy a prescription for success. He was to follow righteousness (that is, to pursue goodness), faith (fidelity to God and people), charity (the Greek word *agape*, meaning love, affection, benevolence), and peace with fellow believers.

Elsewhere, Paul taught the saints in Ephesus to "put off concerning the former conversation the old man, which is corrupt according to the deceitful lusts; and be renewed in the spirit of your mind; and that ye put on the new man, which after God is created in righteousness and true holiness" (Ephesians 4:22–24).

Salvation is a free gift from God, which we accept by simple faith in Jesus Christ. But our growth in grace demands effort on our part. When it comes to unhelpful desires, flee them. Follow after better things. Put off your old nature and put on the new. It isn't easy, but it's vital—and achievable.

Father, help me to put off the old man today and put on the new one. I want to be able to flee all forms of lust.

WHISPERS OF JESUS

The L*ORD* *said unto my Lord, Sit thou at my right hand, until I make thine enemies thy footstool.*

PSALM 110:1

Starting with the *proto evangelium*—the first gospel—of Genesis 3:15, the Bible abounds with hints of a future Savior who would save humanity from its sin. The Psalms are especially rich with dozens of messianic prophecies: A *mashiach* is coming. The promised Anointed One. The Messiah. The Savior.

By Jesus' day, as the Jews suffered under the hands of their Roman overlords, expectations for the Messiah were coming to a boil. So when Jesus entered Jerusalem during His final week, He challenged the Pharisees to identify the Son of David—a popular messianic title of the time. Using the prophecy of Psalm 110:1, Jesus asked them to explain how the Messiah could be David's son when David called the Messiah his "Lord." The Pharisees were stumped. The Old Testament they claimed to know contains scores of messianic prophecies, yet they didn't connect the dots to Jesus.

How about you? The Old Testament evidence confirming Jesus as God's Anointed One is overwhelming. And what was hidden to so many has been fully revealed to us (Colossians 1:26–27). The wise man sees Christ in the Old Testament and rejoices in God's plan to save His people from the beginning.

Lord God, help me to see Jesus in the Old Testament. Please give me a greater understanding and appreciation of Your eternal plan of salvation.

ALL THE HELP YOU NEED

The Holy Ghost shall teach you in the same hour what ye ought to say.
LUKE 12:12

Have you ever started a conversation about Jesus when suddenly you had no idea what to say or how to say it? This condition may be caused by nerves or even a satanic distraction. . .and it's very common.

But God has a solution that's available to each and every one of us. At the very beginning of the church age, Christians were promised a gift—the Holy Spirit would be given to every follower of Jesus as a counselor and guide. The Spirit would step in to pray when we can't string together coherent words for God. He'll do the same when we're discussing our faith in Jesus. But the Holy Spirit will generally draw upon the knowledge of scripture that we already possess.

So spend time learning the rich wisdom of God from His Word. Then you can expect the Spirit to remind you of things you've learned, just as you need them most. He'll help you with the words to speak. He'll speak His wisdom through you.

Lord, I don't have all the answers and I can't always remember everything You've said. Please open my heart to Your Spirit's leading. May He speak through me to share Your truth with the world.

NOT CONSUMED

It is of the LORD's mercies that we are not consumed,
because his compassions fail not.
LAMENTATIONS 3:22

Here's a stark and sobering truth: If God placed judgment on people at the very moment they broke His law, then no human could live beyond their first failed rule. Judgment would fall on each of us, very quickly. This would affect you and every person you care about.

But God makes it clear that His kindness, compassion, mercy, and grace can be trusted. His mercies never fail. And because of that truth, "we are not consumed."

Wisdom is filled with joy knowing that nobody gets what they deserve immediately. We try to compare ourselves to others who seem to break more of God's rules than we do—but God compares our imperfection to *His* perfection and everyone comes up short.

Be happy that God doesn't want to give you what you deserve. His response to all human beings starts with kindness and mercy. Let's accept that blessing and pass it along to others.

Give me the wisdom to embrace mercy, Lord.
Give me the understanding that delayed
judgment makes things better for everyone.

FORGIVING WITHOUT LIMITS

Then came Peter to him, and said, Lord, how oft shall my brother sin against me, and I forgive him? till seven times? Jesus saith unto him, I say not unto thee, Until seven times: but, Until seventy times seven.

MATTHEW 18:21–22

Many of us struggle with forgiving others when they hurt or offend us. But forgiveness becomes a seemingly impossible endeavor when the offenses continue, when someone hurts us repeatedly and unrepentantly.

Peter probably assumed he would impress Jesus by offering to forgive someone seven times. Yes, that would be a good thing to do. But the Twelve were astonished when Jesus said they should forgive others "seventy times seven" times.

That's 490 times! they probably thought. *He can't really mean that!*

But Jesus did mean it. He was calling His followers to a life marked by unlimited forgiveness for others, a life well defined with these words from the apostle Paul: "And be ye kind one to another, tenderhearted, forgiving one another, even as God for Christ's sake hath forgiven you" (Ephesians 4:32).

Wisdom is forgiving others who hurt or offend you—and not just 490 times. Forgive as many times as a person sins against you. . .just the same way God forgives you (1 John 1:9).

Jesus, You have forgiven me for more acts of sin and rebellion than I can possibly count. May I always forgive others, even if they offend or hurt me many times over.

GOD'S NOT CRUEL

I returned, and saw under the sun, that the race is not to the swift, nor the battle to the strong, neither yet bread to the wise, nor yet riches to men of understanding, nor yet favour to men of skill; but time and chance happeneth to them all.

ECCLESIASTES 9:11

Many people overlook Ecclesiastes since it seems to suggest that life is not all sunshine. In fact, this book has the audacity to say that no matter who you are, how powerful you may be, how quickly you run, how rich you are, how skillful or wise you may be—bad things are going to happen.

People like Daniel, Moses, Job, and so many others had experienced this. But many people still believed God only allows good things to come to the righteous. The wise King Solomon saw that hard times were the common ground of *all* people, and he wrote that in his book. People didn't always experience success. Sometimes they were hungry. Sometimes they were poor. In short, human life can be quite disappointing.

Wise men know that bad things happen to even the best of humans. That doesn't make God cruel. Wisdom knows that sometimes God uses our worst circumstances to accomplish the best things—like our salvation and growth in grace.

When hard times seem normal, Lord, remind me that You love me. . .and that I'm never alone.

TRUE WISDOM

For the wisdom of this world is foolishness with God.
For it is written, He taketh the wise in their own craftiness.
1 Corinthians 3:19

Albert Einstein is considered the smartest man who ever lived. But in 1954, he penned these words in a letter: "The word *God* is for me nothing more than the expression and product of human weakness, the Bible a collection of honorable, but still purely primitive, legends which are nevertheless pretty childish. No interpretation, no matter how subtle, can change this for me." Einstein, like so many others, considered himself above the notion of a holy, triune God. But the wisdom of this world is foolishness with God.

"If the Church has no better anchor than the wisdom of this world, then, indeed, will it drift from all its moorings, and be tossed continually upon the seas of ceaseless speculation," wrote the Rev. A. W. Pitzer (1834–1927). The good news is, the church doesn't have to endure this, for God "layeth up sound wisdom for the righteous: he is a buckler to them that walk uprightly" (Proverbs 2:7).

Don't be impressed by worldly wisdom. Instead, fix your gaze upon the Lord and His Word. He will provide you with the true wisdom.

Lord, may I never be impressed by the "wise men" of this world. As 1 Corinthians 1:18 says, "The preaching of the cross is to them that perish foolishness; but unto us which are saved it is the power of God."

LOOK BELOW THE SURFACE

Then the king answered and said unto the woman,
Hide not from me, I pray thee, the thing that I shall ask thee.
And the woman said, Let my lord the king now speak.
And the king said, Is not the hand of Joab with thee in all this?
2 SAMUEL 14:18–19

The story of Absalom's conspiracy against his father, David, is full of intrigue. Perhaps we can draw a spiritual application from the political machinations.

Exceptionally good looking, Absalom was equally selfish. He killed the half brother who violated Absalom's full sister, then ran to another country for refuge. David longed for Absalom, but maintained his banishment—so the king's military commander found someone to spin a story paralleling David's own situation. He quickly recognized the subterfuge, and responded with the words above.

David allowed the return of Absalom, who then began to flatter his countrymen in an attempt to usurp the throne. Soon, a messenger told David, "The hearts of the men of Israel are after Absalom" (2 Samuel 15:13). His rebellion against God's anointed king was ultimately doomed, and his followers would have been wise to look below the surface to the young man's dark purposes.

As Christians, we shouldn't be immediately suspicious of people. But we should recognize that people and situations aren't always as they first appear. Perhaps that's why Jesus once told His disciples to be "wise as serpents, and harmless as doves" (Matthew 10:16).

Lord, give me wise discernment in this world of falsehood.

JESUS' GROWTH MONTAGE

And Jesus increased in wisdom and stature,
and in favour with God and man.
Luke 2:52

A "montage" is a film technique where a series of clips are edited together, often set to music, and used to show the passage of time or repetitive events in a digestible form. If the book of Luke were a film, Luke 2:52 would be shown as a montage.

Sandwiched between Jesus as a boy talking with the Jewish elders and John the Baptist preparing the way for Jesus' adult ministry, this verse might get lost in a daily reading—but it communicates a mind-boggling truth about Jesus.

As God in the flesh, Jesus had all of God's abilities and powers at His disposal. Yet Luke 2:52 shows Him as fully human. Jesus grew up, gaining wisdom and stature and favor—like a normal guy.

If it was possible for Jesus—God incarnate—to grow in wisdom, you have no right to act like a know-it-all. If Jesus went through puberty and grew up physically like the rest of us, He understands humanity at its most awkward level. And if Jesus could grow in favor with God, being God Himself, you must never portray yourself to the world as having arrived spiritually.

Luke 2:52 shows how Jesus became more than He started. He came to make you more too.

Lord, help me grow in wisdom and favor by reading Your Word and becoming like You.

MORE THAN SURVIVING THE MOMENT

O that they were wise, that they understood this,
that they would consider their latter end!
DEUTERONOMY 32:29

Deuteronomy 32 is a message from God. He took a moment to inspire the writing of a passage of sorrow over people who found little use for wisdom. The sixteen words shown above include a powerful takeaway.

You may realize by now that wise people can make great decisions in the here and now—but they also take the end game into account. Wise men look to the future, knowing that whatever choice they make right now will impact what happens in years to come. And even when bad things happen (not even wise men can control that), they simply adjust their decisions. The wise are always looking toward more than just surviving the moment.

God surveyed His people and determined that there were few who were wise, few who understood, and few who really took the time to consider the future. He'd like wise men who can see optimism ahead. Are you one?

Heavenly Father, remind me that You always have answers. And those answers aren't just for today, but for the rest of my life and eternity with You. Help me to do much more than just survive this moment.

THE SAME MIND

Be of the same mind one toward another. Mind not high things, but condescend to men of low estate. Be not wise in your own conceits.
ROMANS 12:16

No doubt, you've had friends or acquaintances who knew too much for their own good. They try to lord their knowledge over everyone else, making them difficult to be around. First Corinthians 8:1 offers this truth: "Knowledge puffeth up, but charity edifieth."

Knowledge without wisdom—that is, knowing how to apply the knowledge—leads to haughtiness. "Smart people" often show disdain for those of lower estate. These include the poor, the illiterate, those weak in their faith or experience, or people who aren't as naturally gifted or talented.

The call in today's verse is to become all things to all people (1 Corinthians 9:22) for their good. Our model is Jesus. He condescended to humankind when He stepped out of heaven and came to earth. He *really* condescended when He willingly allowed Himself to be nailed to a tree for the sins of the world. Now, by setting our own conceits aside, we too can condescend toward the lowly for God's glory.

Lord, whenever I'm tempted to think too highly of myself, remind me that Jesus condescended to me that I might be saved. Give me wisdom so I can learn how to properly apply knowledge.

WISDOM LIKE STARS

And they that be wise shall shine as the brightness of the firmament; and they that turn many to righteousness as the stars for ever and ever.

DANIEL 12:3

Depending on the weather conditions and where you live, a glance at the night sky might reveal a few stars or thousands. A deep black sky splashed with countless vivid stars is awe-inspiring. It might even take your breath away, making you feel very small.

This pictures the impact of wisdom for anyone who pays attention. In the darkness of foolishness, the light of wisdom shines brighter because the contrast is so great. God has allowed us as Christians to understand this truth, but there is always room for growth in our perspective.

Never give up in your pursuit of wisdom. You'll shine brighter as things seem to get darker. And you won't be alone. A wise man is just one among many shining in places where light is most needed. Some lost people will notice, finding themselves attracted to something they can't find in the dark. And you will be doubly blessed.

Thank You for this reminder, Lord. Even when I feel alone in my search for wisdom, I'm shining brightly for someone who's spent too much time in the dark.

CONFRONTATIONAL OR TRANSFORMATIONAL

There arose certain of the synagogue, which is called the synagogue of the Libertines, and Cyrenians, and Alexandrians, and of them of Cilicia and of Asia, disputing with Stephen. And they were not able to resist the wisdom and the spirit by which he spake.

ACTS 6:9–10

Some people hate to be confronted with truth. They either make fun of wisdom or fear it—and often both. They can dismiss the value of sound judgment because it conflicts with the decisions they've made or ones they want to make.

Wisdom seems confrontational and constricting. It can be easy to believe that wisdom and truth are a threat to the status quo. It removes all comfort levels because it makes you think. It can affect the choices that remove you from any appearance of normal.

Stephen was a man of great wisdom. Because of that, he presented a challenge to a whole list of people. These individuals had prepared answers—but Stephen had wisdom. When they couldn't compete with Stephen's wisdom, their reaction was to kill him.

Wisdom can be confrontational. But, when it's accepted, it's transformational.

I don't want to fear wisdom, Father. If the truth is meant to change me then give me the courage to cooperate with the change You want to make in me.

DIVINE MEDICINE

Be not wise in thine own eyes: fear the LORD, and depart from evil. It shall be health to thy navel, and marrow to thy bones.
PROVERBS 3:7–8

Unfortunately, poor health affects us all. It's part of the human condition. Our bodies are temporary. We are subject to disease and atrophy. Part of our eternal life with God includes new bodies (Philippians 3:20–21). But what about now? How do we deal with pain and illness?

Jesus referred to himself as a physician (Mark 2:17) and miraculously healed many physical ailments. Today's verse opens up His doctor's bag and reveals some divine medicine: fear of the Lord and separation from evil.

Fearing God is more than respect, but it's nothing like terror. It's reverence and awe. It's acknowledging that God is the Creator and sustainer. Only He can provide eternal life.

Separating oneself from evil is a natural outcome of pursuing God. It keeps you from physically destructive behavior and frees you to be an instrument for His kingdom (Romans 12:1).

God's Word does not promise perfect health. But today's verse reminds us that wise living and walking in step with God is nourishment for an ailing body.

Lord, help me to trust You when I face physical difficulties. May I always fear You and depart from evil.

UNLIKE REHOBOAM, LISTEN TO WISE MEN

But he forsook the counsel of the old men, which they had given him, and consulted with the young men that were grown up with him, and which stood before him.

1 KINGS 12:8

King Solomon's wisdom was a gift from God. Genetics had nothing to do with it, as his son Rehoboam soon found out after his father's death. Rehoboam's first official act as king? Rejecting wise counsel!

Older is not always better. Young people are not necessarily more foolish. Yet Rehoboam listened to foolish counsel—mostly out of pride and selfishness.

It's not enough to attempt to avoid foolish counsel if you don't know what it is. What does foolish counsel look like? How does wise advice sound?

Rehoboam could have asked these questions before he made a decision that cost him the greater portion of his kingdom. And he could have found the answers in the many wise proverbs his father had penned for him many years before.

Like his idolatrous, foolish father in old age, Rehoboam had no heart for the Lord God. And without the fear of God, there is no beginning to wisdom. All that's left is a mushy mind heeding foolish counsel and reaping terrible consequences.

Lord, may I listen only to those who encourage me to heed Your Word.

THE BETTER EXAMPLE OF WISDOM

He sought God in the days of Zechariah, who had understanding in the visions of God: and as long as he sought the LORD, God made him to prosper.
2 CHRONICLES 26:5

Uzziah became king of Judah when he was sixteen years old. This young man did many things right. There was a good reason for Uzziah's positive actions: a man named Zechariah, whom Uzziah considered a mentor.

It seems Uzziah looked up to Zechariah. This was a wise thing to do since Zechariah was wise. But Uzziah's sights were set too low. He paid attention to a man rather than God. There came a time when Zechariah was no longer in the picture. . .and when Uzziah had no human example to look up to, he began making horrible choices.

It's not wrong to look up to the example of another person. But because they're only human, they'll eventually let you down—even if only by passing away. Be thankful for any good example, but follow the only one that can give wisdom anytime, anywhere. God Himself is waiting to teach you.

There are people I admire, Lord. They seem wise and helpful. But when I want to learn wisdom from the best example ever, remind me to check in with You first.

WISDOM FROM ABOVE

But the wisdom that is from above is first pure,
then peaceable, gentle, and easy to be intreated, full of mercy
and good fruits, without partiality, and without hypocrisy.
JAMES 3:17

If you've ever wondered whether the wisdom you possess is from God or not, the apostle James offers a test: Godly wisdom is pure, peaceable, gentle, easy to be entreated, full of mercy and good fruits, without partiality, and without hypocrisy. That's a much higher standard than the world offers.

"Who is a wise man and endued with knowledge among you?" James wrote earlier. "Let him shew out of a good conversation his works with meekness of wisdom. But if ye have bitter envying and strife in your hearts, glory not, and lie not against the truth. This wisdom descendeth not from above, but is earthly, sensual, devilish" (James 3:13–15).

Worldly understandings of wisdom focus on natural intelligence, deep study, and experience. But the Christian seeks an outside source for his wisdom—that is, God Himself. Then he exhibits the Lord's characteristics in applying it.

Father, I crave the wisdom from above. I want the world around me to see You in anything and everything I say and do.

TROUBLE RESCUE

Who is wise, and he shall understand these things? prudent, and he shall know them? for the ways of the LORD are right, and the just shall walk in them: but the transgressors shall fall therein.

HOSEA 14:9

The wisdom God offers may seem foolish to those who've never been introduced to it. It's not uncommon for people to think that anything discussed in the name of God is ridiculous and irrational. If a person can't believe in God, then anything that's attributed to God may be utterly rejected even when it's the only thing that could rescue a person from the trouble they face.

The plans God has for the world are right, proper, and impressive. His wisdom is unmatched—and it's this wisdom that He offers to you. The wise understand the things God says. The prudent know God's Word. Those who reject God will struggle to stand and may ultimately fall because they reject the only help that's authentically helpful. In doing so, they can't understand and they don't know because they don't want to understand.

The wisdom of God is more than just understanding or knowing—it's doing what a godly wise man should do.

The wise know and understand You. Father, I must believe in You first. Give me a wisdom that starts with belief, improves with trust, and leads me to what You want.

HOLD FAST

Behold, I come quickly: hold that fast which thou hast, that no man take thy crown.

Revelation 3:11

The church in Philadelphia had a commendable reputation—it was the only one of the seven in Asia Minor that Jesus didn't rebuke in some fashion. The Philadelphian believers had a reputation for faithfulness to Christ (Revelation 3:8) and perseverance in the face of trials (verse 10). Jesus had a message for these people: Hold fast to what they'd been doing so no one would take their crown. The Lord wanted them to keep in mind that their hardships wouldn't last forever. Eventually, He would return to make all things right.

If you had to name a few things that define your church's reputation, what would they be? Do those characteristics line up with what the Bible teaches? If so, hold fast to them—practice them, promote them, and give yourself to them. In so doing, you are storing up crowns in heaven. The world may look at your actions and think you are wasting your time. It may even mock you for your faithfulness. But Revelation 3:12 makes the following promise: "Him that overcometh will I make a pillar in the temple of my God. . .and I will write upon him the name of my God. . .and I will write upon him my new name."

Lord, give me the same desire that the Philadelphian believers had—to remain faithful to You.

LIGHT VERSUS HEAT

The words of wise men are heard in quiet more than the cry of him that ruleth among fools.
ECCLESIASTES 9:17

Remember how the prophet Elijah had discovered God's voice in a whisper? In Ecclesiastes, King Solomon described wisdom as something that is shared quietly.

This suggests that there's no need to shout to get your point across. Calm, deliberative discussion just feels more rational and relational, doesn't it? It's less protest and more friendship building—a desire to promote change among those who come to value the calm interaction. Yelling often feels like hatred.

The opposing image that Solomon described is the loud leader of the foolish. This person has things to say, but they're exhausting to hear.

Wisdom always brings light—illumination—to tough issues. Foolishness much prefers heat—that is, controversy. Wisdom calms troubled conversation while foolishness promotes anger.

Isn't it clear what our world needs today?

Show me that I should bring light to my conversations, God. I want to resist the heat of confrontation so I can stay away from foolish words that I'll regret. Please give the wisdom of a cool head and a warm heart.

HONEST WITH GOD

Jesus said unto him, If thou canst believe, all things are possible to him that believeth. And straightway the father of the child cried out, and said with tears, Lord, I believe; help thou mine unbelief.

MARK 9:23–24

In today's passage, the father of a demon-possessed boy comes to Jesus, desperately seeking help. After Jesus assures the man that "all things are possible to him that believeth," the man makes a tearful—and curious—confession: "Lord, I believe; help thou mine unbelief."

Seems like a bit of a contradiction, doesn't it? Some things people say in scripture invite us in to get inside that person's head and read between the lines of their words. Perhaps this man truly believed Jesus *could* help the boy, but waffled on whether the Lord *would*.

The most important thing here is that Jesus responded to the man's confession. The Lord rebuked the evil spirit, commanding it to leave the boy. It obeyed with a shriek, leaving the child crumpled on the ground. But Jesus helped him back to his feet—completely healed.

Can you relate to this man's struggle? Do you know that God can do good in your life but wonder if He will? If so, you'd be wise not to pretend otherwise. Speak honestly with Jesus. He will honor your tiny faith and help your unbelief.

Lord Jesus, help me to believe You always, even when unbelief troubles my mind. Remind me that I can—and should—always be honest with You.

WISDOM EQUALS PATIENCE

David behaved himself wisely in all his ways;
and the LORD was with him.
1 SAMUEL 18:14

Wouldn't it be strange if 1 Samuel 18:14 read, "David behaved himself wisely in some of his ways; and he didn't need God's help"? Sure, it sounds ridiculous—but many men think they can be wise without God's help.

Wisdom can be confused with common sense. While there are similarities, wisdom is more than just responding to normal human experiences in a helpful way.

The wisdom described in 1 Samuel 18 relates to the way David chose to respond to King Saul's jealousy. David didn't retaliate. In fact, he sought the good of a king whom God said he would replace, even when Saul was trying to kill him. David refused to rush the process.

David was so wise that he had to talk sense into men who were faithful to him, aggressive guys who wanted to overthrow King Saul on David's behalf. But the younger man knew that he would become king when God decided it was time. To David, behaving himself wisely looked a lot like being patient.

I'm not always as patient as I should be, God. But I know that Your plans and timetable are far better than my own. Please teach me patience in Your wisdom.

GREATNESS

The queen of the south shall rise up in the judgment with this generation, and shall condemn it: for she came from the uttermost parts of the earth to hear the wisdom of Solomon; and, behold, a greater than Solomon is here.

MATTHEW 12:42

You probably remember one major thing about King Solomon: He was known as the wisest man on earth. But that wasn't anything natural or accidental: Solomon's wisdom was a gift from God. He was renowned for his incredible mental abilities, but Solomon wasn't just wise—by God's grace, he was also extraordinarily rich.

When Jesus arrived on earth, He was not recognized for His wisdom. He was certainly not rich. And yet Matthew recorded that Jesus was greater than Solomon.

How? Jesus didn't need a gift of wisdom—it had originated with Him. Though He appeared to be poor, He actually owned the entire universe. His actual godhood, His rescue plan for sinful humanity, His love and humility all took Jesus to a level of greatness that will never be rivaled.

Now, each of us can be part of this greatness by simple faith. When we believed and followed Jesus, God "raised us up together, and made us sit together in heavenly places in Christ Jesus: that in the ages to come he might shew the exceeding riches of his grace in his kindness toward us through Christ Jesus" (Ephesians 2:6–7).

I want this kind of greatness, Lord—make me wise enough to follow Jesus by simple faith every day.

WISDOM IN REPENTANCE

Have mercy upon me, O God, according to thy lovingkindness: according unto the multitude of thy tender mercies blot out my transgressions.

PSALM 51:1

David had just committed the most egregious sins of his life. In a shocking display of lust, pride, deception, and violence, the great Israelite king committed adultery with his friend Uriah's wife, Bathsheba. Then, when David found out she was pregnant, he tried to cover up his sin before ultimately arranging Uriah's death in battle.

After being confronted by the prophet Nathan, David was convicted of his terrible transgressions. And being the talented lyricist that he was, he penned a beautiful song of confession and repentance, Psalm 51.

Once convicted, David didn't shy away from his sin. He took full ownership of it and cried out to God for mercy and grace.

May we do the same! Thanks to Jesus' great sacrifice on our behalf, our sins no longer condemn us when we trust in Him (Romans 8:1). We must never presume upon God's grace. But if we sin, running toward grace in humble contrition and repentance will always bring full forgiveness. "If we confess our sins, he is faithful and just to forgive us our sins, and to cleanse us from all unrighteousness" (1 John 1:9).

Heavenly Father, I'm sorry for my sins against You and others. In Your great lovingkindness, please forgive me and create in me a clean heart.

WHERE TO FIND THE TRUTH THAT MAKES YOU FREE

Then said Jesus to those Jews which believed on him, If ye continue in my word, then are ye my disciples indeed; and ye shall know the truth, and the truth shall make you free.

John 8:31–32

It's easy to accept the wisdom of John 8:32, "And ye shall know the truth, and the truth shall make you free." Motivational posters, Christian art, and T-shirts all highlight these words. This thought, on its own, might even lead some to assume that truth just magically shows up. That's not actually true, so you'll need to ask where exactly truth is found.

Real wisdom knows that truth is found in God's Word. If you're a disciple of Jesus (and we certainly hope that's true) then keep reading, studying, and thinking about what He has said in the pages of the Bible.

But don't just consume a few nuggets of wisdom and assume you know everything you need to know. True disciples, committed followers of Jesus, stay in the Word. They think about what they're learning. And then they share that with others.

I want to know truth, Lord. I want the freedom that Your truth brings. Please keep me in Your Word and explain it to my heart.

PRIORITY LISTS

He hath shewed thee, O man, what is good; and what doth the LORD *require of thee, but to do justly, and to love mercy, and to walk humbly with thy God?*

MICAH 6:8

Men seem to like priority lists. Either in our minds or on paper, we note the things we want to accomplish, in the order we think best. The big question is whether our priority lists correspond with God's plans for us.

If you'd like to check the alignment of your priority list with God's, pay special attention to today's scripture. Through the prophet Micah, God described His most important goals for us: First, pursue justice. That just means doing what's right according to God's Word. Next, love mercy. We should prefer kindness and love to anger and unforgiveness. Finally, walk humbly with God. That means we must never allow ourselves to think we know more than He does.

Wisdom seeks to align our goals with God's priorities. And He's made the list simple—only three elements! Look at everything you do through the prism of Micah 6:8, and you will inevitably make wiser choices.

Lord God, I know that You want to be included in my decision making. Please remind me every day to talk with You about my plans. And help me to prioritize justice, mercy, and humility.

BAD COMPANY

Be not deceived: evil communications corrupt good manners.

1 Corinthians 15:33

John Wesley's understanding of today's verse is that the apostle Paul quoted the Greek playwright Menander (around 342–292 BC) in this verse. Menander's work *Thais*, which is now lost to us except for a few fragments, contained something wise enough to share with the believers of Corinth—and by extension, all of us. Paul used elements from the broader culture to communicate Christian truths effectively, in this case combatting false teachings about resurrection.

Modern Bible translations often use the phrase "bad company" rather than "evil communications." Either way, the message is clear: Spending too much time with negative influences is unwise—it will corrupt virtuous habits and good character. But the converse is also true. Time spent with the family of God supports the growth of personal goodness (Proverbs 13:20).

It's all about intentionality. Be careful who you spend your time with, because you will often end up just like them.

Lord, give me the wisdom to surround myself with strong believers so that my character will not be corrupted. And may I help others to shape their character in positive ways.

THE GRASS ISN'T ALWAYS GREENER

For I was envious at the foolish, when I saw the prosperity of the wicked.
PSALM 73:3

Ever wondered why you should pursue a life of righteousness when all around you evil people are flourishing?

Or forget the blatantly wicked for a moment and consider the regular folks next door—the seemingly happy, non-religious family with the big house, well-manicured lawn, roomy SUV, three bubbly kids, and a vacation home at the beach. They aren't pursuing the Lord, but they seem to be so happy, so put together, so "with it." They appear to have everything anyone could want. Is following the Lord really worth it? Does it really matter?

Asaph, a chief musician during the reign of King David, wondered this too. He admitted to being "envious at the foolish," and he desired "the prosperity of the wicked" (Psalm 73:3). When he pondered all this, "it was too painful for me," he admitted, "until I went into the sanctuary of God; then understood I their end" (verses 16–17).

And there's the kicker. What we put our trust in and pursue in this life *does* matter because it directly affects our eternity. Asaph realized that pursuing temporal worldly gain is folly, but "it is good for me to draw near to God" (verse 28).

Have you discovered this wisdom yourself?

Lord, please help me not pursue the things of this world. Make me wise enough to pursue You alone.

THE DEPTH OF GOD'S RICHES

O the depth of the riches both of the wisdom and knowledge of God! how unsearchable are his judgments, and his ways past finding out!
ROMANS 11:33

Learn all you can—and you'll discover it won't be enough. Think long and hard about things you care about—you'll find you're still missing something. But ask God for wisdom—and you'll learn that He's ready to teach. What you'll gain will be deep, rich, and extravagant. Expect joy with each new discovery.

A precept is a rule designed to regulate actions. God's Word is filled with them. On their own, these thoughts are helpful and often quoted, but they serve a larger purpose, with a bigger picture to consider. When God answers your prayer for wisdom, He also helps you discover the links between His precepts. You'll begin to see how they all fit together. You may even get to the place where you understand *why* God wants you to obey His rules—even the ones that don't make sense to you now.

On your own, you'll lose your way. But with the Holy Spirit's help, you get direction that moves you ever closer to "the depth of the riches both of the wisdom and knowledge of God."

Lord God, please guide me into the depth of the riches of Your wisdom and knowledge. I want to be as excited by them as the apostle Paul was.

NOTEWORTHY EVENTS

Behold, the LORD passed by, and a great and strong wind rent the mountains, and brake in pieces the rocks before the LORD; but the LORD was not in the wind: and after the wind an earthquake; but the LORD was not in the earthquake: and after the earthquake a fire; but the LORD was not in the fire: and after the fire a still small voice.

1 KINGS 19:11–12

Elijah was a messenger who took his job seriously. Sometimes when God delivered a message for him to share it was given in less than expected ways.

If you're not familiar with this story, then you should know that Elijah was waiting to hear from God. In the waiting he experienced three noteworthy events. There was a devastating wind, an earthquake, and a fire. These phenomena might have led Elijah to believe each was part of God's message, but it wasn't. It was a whisper that delivered God's wisdom.

It's easy to think that God's voice comes in noisy events. But sometimes the thing He wants you to know most is shared when all is quiet—when your attention isn't diverted by distressing and depressing news.

God wants your undivided attention. In these moments He can pass along very personal messages with very personal impact.

Lord, please help me to be still enough to hear Your quiet voice. I need to pay attention when the noise of life threatens to distract me once more.

BE OF GOOD CHEER

But when they saw him walking upon the sea, they supposed it had been a spirit, and cried out: for they all saw him, and were troubled. And immediately he talked with them, and saith unto them, Be of good cheer: it is I; be not afraid.

Mark 6:49–50

Think about the things in this world that have the potential to frighten you. In recent years, international events have threatened to escalate to the point where some fear the outbreak of World War III. Then there is economic uncertainty and what it could mean to you and your family. And, of course, the pandemic drama reminds us that microbes—and our society's response to them—can threaten both health and liberty.

It's a scary world. But as followers of Jesus Christ, we can take comfort in the fact that our God is in control. He is bigger than any of the things that frighten us.

Jesus showed His disciples that they could overcome their fears simply by focusing on the fact that He was with them.

When you find yourself struggling with fear, wisdom says, "Jesus sees and cares." And wisdom knows that He will never leave you alone in your fears.

Lord, I know I'll have to face frightening things in this world. But when You're with me, I don't have to give in to fear. Help me to always keep my eyes on You.

CHOOSING TO REST

For in six days the L*ORD made heaven and earth, the sea, and all that in them is, and rested the seventh day: wherefore the* L*ORD blessed the sabbath day, and hallowed it.*

EXODUS 20:11

In the beginning, God was incredibly busy. He made the earth, stars, and planets, and everything in and around them. He made the sea and all that call it home. He made all the plants and everything that would eat them. He made humans and then. . .He rested.

God's wisdom in creation suggests it's reasonable to resist working every single day of your life. You, as a man made in God's image, need refreshment. Your creativity will be enhanced by a time of rest.

You might believe that refusing time off makes you a more valuable employee. You might argue that it increases your personal wealth. But even if that's true, there's a tradeoff that might leave other areas of your life poorer.

A time of rest isn't punishment. A time of rest is the reasonable wisdom that God demonstrated in the magnificent beginning, the time when He created everything you know. And He chose to *rest* when He was done.

Lord God, I'll need Your wisdom to simply rest. Remind me that no earthly task is so important that it supersedes Your example and command of resting.

WISE ENOUGH TO AVOID GOSSIP

Lord, who shall abide in thy tabernacle? who shall dwell in thy holy hill? He that walketh uprightly, and worketh righteousness, and speaketh the truth in his heart. He that backbiteth not with his tongue, nor doeth evil to his neighbour, nor taketh up a reproach against his neighbour.

Psalm 15:1–3

When most Christians think of the "big sins," their minds go to things like murder, adultery, and stealing. The sin of gossip usually doesn't register as being all that serious. The Bible, however, says otherwise.

God takes the things we say to and about others very seriously. That's why the apostle James wrote, "If any man among you seem to be religious, and bridleth not his tongue, but deceiveth his own heart, this man's religion is vain" (James 1:26).

A man who controls his speech and avoids gossip is a wise man indeed. He's a man who refuses to speak ill of others—even when what he might otherwise say is true.

Your words have tremendous power to help or to hurt others. So when you talk to or about someone, make sure you say only things that build up and hearten, not tear down or discourage.

Father, thank You for providing guidelines and commands for living a life that pleases You. I will commit myself to making sure that I speak only words that encourage others and avoid critical speech, which only tears down what You are working to build up.

ANGER UNDER CONTROL

He that is slow to anger is better than the mighty;
and he that ruleth his spirit than he that taketh a city.
PROVERBS 16:32

Can you imagine taking control of an enemy city? Think of the skills you would need to lead your troops to victory. Consider the energy you would expend fighting, controlling enemy territory, and eventually governing that place. God called Joshua to take many cities as the Israelites conquered Canaan (Joshua 1–12). David and his "mighty men" did many similar things with God's blessing (2 Samuel 23:8–39).

Yet, today's verse reveals that God wants more than mighty warriors. God also seeks men who can control their anger. As Paul would later write, God needs men who are so in tune with the Spirit that they are "longsuffering" (Galatians 5:22). Or, as this proverb puts it, "slow to anger."

Proverbs 16:32 is one of many "better than" verses in the Bible. "Better than" is God's way of saying, "Yes, sometimes I need warriors. But most of the time, I need patient men. I need men with self-control." Fighting through enemy lines and ruling a city would take enormous effort and skill. Yet God values the man who is patient and self-disciplined even more.

Lord, please forgive me for the times my anger controls me. Help me to grow the spiritual fruit of self-control.

THE ONLY ONE TO CONSULT

Where is the wise? where is the scribe? where is the disputer of this world? hath not God made foolish the wisdom of this world?

1 CORINTHIANS 1:20

When God speaks, it's not the start of a debate—at least not a winnable one. Is this a challenge anyone could take on? Is even the wisest man wiser than God? Is an author smarter than the God who created words?

God's wisdom is unique because it operates outside conventional experience. His wisdom often contradicts what usually makes sense to us. God's wisdom is fully aware of what works, and He never needs to consult with any human being to determine if His way will work. On the other hand, when you consult with Him, you'll always leave with something to consider about personal behavior and choices.

Feel free to go to God believing you're wise enough to argue your own point. But know that you'll be talking to the all-knowing Creator of all things. His wisdom never changes. He'll listen to your opinion, but your opinion will never change His truth.

I want a life that makes sense to You, God.
Help me to learn so it makes sense to me too.
I need Your wisdom to know the best way to live.

"IF POSSIBLE"

For Paul had determined to sail by Ephesus, because he would not spend the time in Asia: for he hasted, if it were possible for him, to be at Jerusalem the day of Pentecost.
Acts 20:16

Exactly where human decision-making and God's sovereignty intersect is a topic far beyond the scope of this devotional. It's enough to say that the two ideas exist side by side in God's Word.

The phrase "if it were possible" in today's scripture parallels a common interjection—"Lord willing"—that arises from the book of James: "Go to now, ye that say, To day or to morrow we will go into such a city, and continue there a year, and buy and sell, and get gain: Whereas ye know not what shall be on the morrow. For what is your life? It is even a vapour, that appeareth for a little time, and then vanisheth away. For that ye ought to say, *If the Lord will*, we shall live, and do this, or that" (4:13–15, emphasis added).

You are free to make your own plans, though it's wise to hold them loosely. Always add an "If possible" or "Lord willing," spoken or otherwise, to acknowledge God's higher authority in your life. He may overrule your pursuits for His own wise reasons. . .as a loving, all-knowing Father who has His son's best interests at heart.

Lord, I ask You to oversee my plans, and overrule them as necessary. I trust You to guide me into the best paths.

OPEN EARS

That the communication of thy faith may become effectual by the acknowledging of every good thing which is in you in Christ Jesus.
PHILEMON 6

Philemon, a wealthy man from Colosse, was one of Paul's converts. In this short letter, Paul addressed a hard topic: The great apostle wanted Philemon to take back his escaped slave Onesimus. In fact, Paul asked Philemon to receive Onesimus in the same manner in which he would receive the apostle himself. Paul appealed to Philemon's love toward the saints, asking God to make Philemon's ministry (even more) effectual.

When you have to say something difficult to a fellow believer, following Paul's example here would be wise. Speak softly. Look for common ground on which you can build a bridge. Acknowledge the gospel you see at work in the other person. Mention specific ways you are praying for his or her ministry to prosper for God's glory. And then make your appeal.

By not focusing solely on the point of contention, the other person is more likely to genuinely hear what you have to say. This may also prevent Satan from gaining a foothold in the relationship.

Lord, give me eyes to see the gospel at work in the lives of other believers. Remind me to compliment that, even when I have something hard I need to communicate.

WALK WITH THE WISE

He that walketh with wise men shall be wise:
but a companion of fools shall be destroyed.
PROVERBS 13:20

Some biblical principles are easier to live by than others. Today's scripture is one of them.

While God will always provide the strength we need to do what He says, certain duties require a lot of faith. Shadrach, Meshach, and Abednego couldn't have stood tall in that crowd of prostrate Babylonians without some serious commitment to their Lord.

But walking with the wise? That's easy.

If you want to be wise, just make sure you're hanging out with the right crowd. Look for other Christian guys who have a clear passion for the Lord and His Word. In this world, they'll be pretty obvious. . .and because they are wise, they'll be happy to include you in their lives. True Christianity is never an exclusive club.

As you walk with the wise, the proverbs say you'll become wise. Then you can pass your wisdom along to other Christian guys, who will in turn do that for others. On and on the cycle goes until Jesus returns.

Really, it's a pretty ingenious system. But wouldn't you expect that from our all-wise God?

Heavenly Father, I want to be wise. Please lead me to wise men with whom I can walk. . .then help me to pass along the wisdom I gain to others.

LET YOUR LIGHT SHINE!

Neither do men light a candle, and put it under a bushel, but on a candlestick; and it giveth light unto all that are in the house. Let your light so shine before men, that they may see your good works, and glorify your Father which is in heaven.

MATTHEW 5:15–16

Have you ever heard this question posed about your Christian witness: "If you were arrested for being a Christian, would there be enough evidence to convict you?" Another way to pose that question might be, in the (paraphrased) words of Jesus, "Are you letting your light shine before others?"

For various reasons, we Christian men often don't succeed in letting the light of Christ shine out from inside us into the world. The good news, however, is that we still have the opportunity to do just that, starting today.

Jesus is the true Light of the World (see John 8:12), and when we come to Him in faith, He fills us with His Spirit so that we can grow in Him and become more and more like Him every day. When that happens, His light shines from inside us out into the world.

So make sure you don't put a bushel over your candle. Let that light shine for all to see!

Jesus, I want Your light to shine from my heart and out into the world so that God the Father will be glorified.

BEST EFFORTS. . .INSPIRED

Thou hast also given me the shield of thy salvation: and thy gentleness hath made me great.
2 SAMUEL 22:36

When David prayed, he admitted that he believed he could do nothing good on his own. Of course God didn't need this reminder, but it was important that David himself arrived at this conclusion. It was important that he prayed this prayer. It was important that the king believed.

It's easy to take credit for things that seem to be the result of our own personal efforts. We might even feel as if an "attaboy" is in order when we complete a project and it turns out well. King David provided a template response. That response is that good things are God things. Your best efforts were inspired by the God who gave all good things.

King David had often witnessed moments when God intervened in his affairs. It always turned out better when this earthly king allowed the King of Heaven to readjust his plans. Wisdom suggests that the earthly king was right about the heavenly King. Wisdom also suggests that you can note David's response and choose to do the same.

When something I do is noticed, Father, I want to notice You. I want to thank You. Help me to remember that nothing good is possible without You.

RESISTING DECEIVERS

Look to yourselves, that we lose not those things which we have wrought, but that we receive a full reward.
2 John 8

In writing to the elect lady and her children, the apostle John expressed joy over their faith and love, then transitioned to cautioning them about deceivers. "For many deceivers are entered into the world, who confess not that Jesus Christ is come in the flesh. This is a deceiver and an antichrist" (2 John 7). John wanted this family to take care of themselves by being aware that they would encounter deceivers and their false doctrines.

It's wise for believers today to be aware of the same issue, for Satan is at work. Jesus warned about this: "For there shall arise false Christs, and false prophets, and shall shew great signs and wonders; insomuch that, if it were possible, they shall deceive the very elect" (Matthew 24:24). One sure way to do this is feast on the Word of God so you'll know error when you hear it. Hebrews 5:14 says, "But strong meat [a steady diet of scripture] belongeth to them that are of full age, even those who by reason of use have their senses exercised to discern both good and evil."

Lord, help me to watch after myself so I'm not susceptible to the evil one. Give me a strong appetite for the Word so I will know a deceiver when he speaks.

NUMBERING OUR DAYS

Teach us to number our days, that we may apply our hearts unto wisdom.
PSALM 90:12

Scripture is always realistic, pragmatic, and honest—often bluntly so. For all of our pride, vanity, and feelings of self-sufficiency, we humans really are quite small and unimpressive. And the Bible tells us so.

Psalm 90, the only entry of Moses in the Psalms, is one of those scriptures that slaps us with a reality check. It points out one of many differences between God and us: God is eternal and created everything. He is outside time. A thousand years is like a tick on the clock to Him.

As for us? Well, we humans will be here on earth for a whopping seventy years. Eighty if we're fortunate. Relatively speaking, we're not much different than green grass that fades by nightfall.

While this is sobering, the Bible doesn't want us to walk away feeling forlorn. Rather, Moses redirects our attention to the all-important correlate in Psalm 90:12, telling us to "number our days" to achieve a heart of wisdom.

"Numbering our days" isn't a countdown toward death. It's a call to action. Moses, under the Holy Spirit's inspiration, is saying, "Human life on this earth is short, so be wise with the time you've graciously been given. Make the most of it for God's glory."

God, please help me number my days and live wisely for Your glory.

SIN IS ILLOGICAL

Much people of the Jews therefore knew that he was there: and they came not for Jesus' sake only, but that they might see Lazarus also, whom he had raised from the dead. But the chief priests consulted that they might put Lazarus also to death; because that by reason of him many of the Jews went away, and believed on Jesus.

John 12:9–11

Does it make any sense for the Jewish chief priests to plot to kill a guy Jesus had already brought back from the dead? This odd vignette in the book of John illustrates how illogical sin is—and makes us.

We've all been tempted to do things we clearly know are wrong, foolish, dumb. And yet, at times, we've all given in. This is a sad reality of life in a broken world, even though we've been saved and changed by Jesus.

The apostle Paul also felt that crazy internal tug-of-war. "For that which I do I allow not," he wrote, "for what I would, that do I not; but what I hate, that do I" (Romans 7:15).

Paul recognized the only answer to his problem was God's grace through Jesus Christ. Though his body craved wrong, Paul's mind could pursue a deeper, more loving and obedient relationship with his Lord (Romans 7:24–25).

That was something the Jewish leaders of Jesus' day steadfastly refused. May we never allow ourselves to wander down that illogical path.

Lord, make me wise and keep me true to You.

A MINIMIZED IMPACT

Therefore will the LORD wait, that he may be gracious unto you, and therefore will he be exalted, that he may have mercy upon you: for the LORD is a God of judgment: blessed are all they that wait for him.

ISAIAH 30:18

Judgment is coming! Judgment is coming! It can sound like a call from a horseback rider alerting all to impending doom. This verse from Isaiah confirms that God is a God of justice so it's safe to heed the warning, "Judgment is coming!"

But before you ever witness judgment there's a decision that God makes first, and He has a purpose for making it. When you break His rules, and when you witness lawbreaking, there are two actions God takes before He chooses to judge. The first is that God chooses to be gracious to sinners. The second is that He chooses to be merciful.

God is paying attention and He doesn't overlook broken laws, but you can rejoice knowing that grace and mercy are the kind actions of a God who loves you. People who are willing to wait for God's kindness to minimize the impact of justice are called blessed.

Be blessed.

I can be happy choosing Your grace, God. But I can look at others and wish You would show them judgment. Help me to gladly wait for justice and champion Your mercy for everyone.

OVERCOMING EVIL

Be not overcome of evil, but overcome evil with good.
ROMANS 12:21

Watchman Nee was imprisoned for his faith in 1952 during the Communist takeover of China and spent the last twenty years of his life behind bars. He once wrote about two Chinese terrace farmers who were at odds with one another. The farmer who owned the field higher on a hill was a Christian; the farmer at the lower level was not. The Christian rose early each morning to pump water by hand for his crops, but his neighbor cut a path through the Christian's dikes so the water would flow to his own field.

As upset as the Christian farmer was, he decided to pump water first for his neighbor's field, then his own. After falling under conviction for his actions, the farmer who wasn't a Christian, eventually apologized and listened to the Christian farmer share the gospel with him. The man bowed his knee before Christ and became a believer.

Injustices can lead to gospel opportunities. What evil are you currently experiencing? Will you agree to pray for a way to overcome evil with good in this situation? If you aren't sure how to do so, pray about that too.

Lord, give me the wisdom and the will to overcome evil with good today.

THE SKILL AND WISDOM LINK

He hath filled him with the spirit of God, in wisdom, in understanding, and in knowledge, and in all manner of workmanship.

Exodus 35:31

The man was known as "Bezaleel the son of Uri, the son of Hur, of the tribe of Judah" (Exodus 35:30). Not many sermons are preached about him, but God made sure His Word recorded five attributes of Bezaleel. He had the Spirit of God; he was wise; he understood hard things; he was smart; and he had some impressive skills.

In many places in the Bible, wisdom is closely linked to the work a man did—his skills. In many cases skill and wisdom could be used interchangeably. Maybe this has to do with the fact that by learning a skill you've proven to be teachable. Wisdom requires the same teachable spirit and includes the understanding needed to apply what you've learned to the plan God has for you in the world around you.

College degrees don't necessarily make a man wise. Working with his hands doesn't preclude wisdom. In fact, in His paradoxical way of doing things, God often turns the conventional wisdom on its head.

I want to be wise enough to work and learn a skill, Father. I also want to be wise enough to follow You and learn to do what You want. Help me to become wise.

FOLLOW JESUS' EXAMPLE

For even the Son of man came not to be ministered unto, but to minister, and to give his life a ransom for many.
MARK 10:45

One of the sinful attitudes in fallen humanity is selfishness. We men tend to want the highest position, the most-respected titles, and whatever gives us the advantage.

Take the example of the brothers James and John, two of Jesus' closest friends among the twelve disciples. They started quite a kerfuffle between themselves and the other ten when they asked Jesus for a high place in His kingdom (see Mark 10:35–41). James and John had made what can only be seen as a selfish request, and the rest of the disciples expressed their displeasure. It wasn't a good look for any of the disciples, but Jesus used James and John's request to teach all twelve an important lesson—namely that they should follow *His* example of perfect servanthood.

Jesus is the King of kings and Lord of lords. But He told the disciples that He hadn't come to earth to be served—rather, to serve and to willingly give up His own life as a ransom so that many could live forever.

It's easy to pursue the wrong things in this life. But we have Jesus' command and example to follow—and His Spirit's wisdom to enable our obedience.

Lord Jesus, help me to follow the perfect example You set as a servant who put others first.

A COMMON DYNAMIC

Wherefore now let the fear of the LORD be upon you; take heed and do it: for there is no iniquity with the LORD our God, nor respect of persons, nor taking of gifts.

2 CHRONICLES 19:7

Jehoshaphat was a much-admired king in Judah. He put laws in place to reflect what he'd learned from God. He legislated with a wisdom grounded in understanding what God was asking of His people. As the leader of God's people, Jehoshaphat thought it was important to urge the people to do what God was asking him to do.

Jehoshaphat showed that he was impartial. He wasn't asking more of the people than he was willing to do himself. God doesn't show partiality; you can't buy Him off; and He'll never break His own rules.

There's wisdom in the leader of a home, community, or nation embracing this dynamic. You discover equality when everyone is treated the same. Equality doesn't demand to be better than others, nor does it expect to be worse.

Wisdom always works to bring balance to the treatment of people based on God's directive to love. King Jehoshaphat did his best to remind the people of Judah that this was what God wanted.

Treating people fairly was Your idea, God. Maybe it's because You knew that most people would place someone on a pedestal and treat others poorly. Help me to remember this was never Your plan.

TEACHABLE

The ear that heareth the reproof of life abideth among the wise.
Proverbs 15:31

Are you teachable, or do you secretly think you know it all? When someone asks for an opinion, do you assume it's *your* opinion he's seeking? Being the smartest man in the room can work. . .as long as you are, in fact, the smartest man in the room. But there will come a time when you encounter someone with more knowledge and understanding.

God's wisdom suggests that you should spend more time learning and listening than you do sharing your own perceived brilliance.

You are on your way to wisdom when you understand that there is always more to learn. And for everything you learn, there's even more to explore about what you have discovered. This is why reading through the Bible is an excellent idea and reading through it more than once is an even better idea. Each reading allows you to see things you may have missed before. That is how you gain more and more understanding of the truths of God's written Word.

Wake up excited that this is a day when you can learn more, share more, and do more because you've chosen to follow God on this most wonderful adventure of gaining knowledge and understanding.

Keep teaching while You help me learn, Father. There will always be something more to discover because You always have more to teach me. Make me teachable.

THE SACRED OIL OF UNITY

Behold, how good and how pleasant it is for brethren to dwell together in unity!
PSALM 133:1

The last time you had a great bro weekend—perhaps camping and hiking, heading to the beach, or watching a big sporting event—you undoubtedly told your buddies, "Guys, we've got to do that again soon. My soul hasn't been that refreshed since I last had oil dripping from my head and into my beard." Right?

Well, that's how David analogizes the sweetness of godly unity in Psalm 133. He describes it as "the precious ointment upon the head, that ran down upon the beard, even Aaron's beard: that went down to the skirts of his garments" (verse 2).

While this metaphor might be obscure to us, it's a reference to a very specific and expensive anointing oil that ancient Israel used to consecrate the high priest, the tabernacle, the ark of the covenant, and other elements used in worshipping the Lord (Exodus 30:22–33). The point: It is a sweet, sacred thing when true believers unite together in proper worship of a holy God.

Don't many of our churches need this today? If you seek to live wisely before God, pursue unity within the body of Christ. Lead where needed, but always in humility, putting others first. Serve others as Christ served us. Forgive and ask for forgiveness when needed.

Christian unity is essential! (Head and beard oil optional.)

Heavenly Father, please unify me and my fellow brothers and sisters in Christ.

TRICKS OF THE HEART

The heart is deceitful above all things,
and desperately wicked: who can know it?
JEREMIAH 17:9

The condition of the human heart has been debated for a very long time. Some suggest it's basically good and should be referred to this way. Others say it can be reformed with time and intention. Then God, in His wisdom, points to Jeremiah 17 and speaks truth. The human heart will deceive you. It's filled with wickedness and the ways of the heart are hard to understand.

This idea might challenge the way you think about your heart, the core of who you are. If you believe it's basically good then you run the risk of disappointment and defeat when you either betray or are betrayed. This is true when you know the right choice to make and refuse to make it. This can also show up when you think someone will stand with you and they walk away.

Wisdom knows the heart plays tricks. It seems to be amused by your response to its suggestions. Following your heart may be the most foolish idea you can believe.

Your heart is perfect, God. It's not deceitful or wicked. It provides wisdom and expresses love. Help me to believe Your answers are worth more than how I feel about anything.

GOSPEL CENTRALITY

Only let your conversation be as it becometh the gospel of Christ: that whether I come and see you, or else be absent, I may hear of your affairs, that ye stand fast in one spirit, with one mind striving together for the faith of the gospel.

PHILIPPIANS 1:27

The apostle Paul wrote his letter to the Philippians while sitting in a Roman prison. He had hopes of visiting the church in Philippi again, but while he was away, he wanted Christians to speak to one another as it became the gospel of Christ. In other words, he didn't want them to depend on him as the minister of the gospel. Whether he was there or not, he wanted them to be united in striving for the faith of the gospel.

When you meet other Christians away from church, what do you talk about? Sports? Weather? Your backyard grilling skills? Does the conversation ever wander into gospel territory?

How might you be more intentional in the future? You might ask the other person which book of the Bible he's currently reading, or what his favorite memory verse is, or even how he overcame a besetting sin. Then let the gospel have its way in your conversation.

Lord, help me to be more intentional about gospel centrality in my conversations this week with fellow believers.

WISDOM IS MERCY

Know therefore that the Lord thy God, he is God, the faithful God, which keepeth covenant and mercy with them that love him and keep his commandments to a thousand generations.
Deuteronomy 7:9

How long can God wait before He brings ultimate justice to a lawbreaking world? God doesn't break His covenant. No, our faithful God waits for mankind to turn to Him and away from the choices that have caused generational destruction.

There are always consequences for breaking God's law, but His mercy works to restore broken relationships, improve personal thinking, and increase a willingness to obey. God's kindness offers course correction to those who follow Him and to inspire those who've yet to make that choice.

Knowledge will always suggest action when personal rights are violated. Wisdom recommends forgiveness and love because God's mercy delays justice for those who need a little more time to come to terms with following.

Mercy may sometimes look like a divine time-out, unfortunate circumstances, or even personal loss. This may be less justice and more an invitation to recognize the God who knows how much You need Him.

I can keep doing things the way I want, Father. I have that choice. But Your mercy offers new opportunities to recognize You and follow where You're leading.

THE WISDOM PRAYER

[I] cease not to give thanks for you, making mention of you in my prayers; that the God of our Lord Jesus Christ, the Father of glory, may give unto you the spirit of wisdom and revelation in the knowledge of him: the eyes of your understanding being enlightened; that ye may know what is the hope of his calling, and what the riches of the glory of his inheritance in the saints, and what is the exceeding greatness of his power to us-ward who believe, according to the working of his mighty power.

Ephesians 1:16–19

Do you pray for others? They need it. This passage in Ephesians 1 explains a good prayer you probably aren't praying. It might read, "Dear God, give my friends and family a spirit of wisdom. Reveal yourself to them whether they know You or not. May they see and understand what is impossible on their own. Help them to understand that You're for them and have a purpose for what You want them to be. Amen."

This is a wisdom prayer. It means you've come to understand the workings of God to such a degree that you want the wisdom you've experienced to fill others as well.

I don't want to ask for wisdom only for myself, Lord—I want this same wisdom for everyone I know. I ask for a society that can experience the value in compassion, sharing, praying for others, and following You.

WISE STEWARDS

For unto every one that hath shall be given,
and he shall have abundance: but from him that hath
not shall be taken away even that which he hath.
MATTHEW 25:29

On the first read-through, today's verse seems inherently unfair. Take from the poor and give to the rich? Really?

Well, no. What today's verse refers to is using our gifts wisely. Go back and read the passage from which it was taken (Matthew 25:14–30). The master of the house entrusts his servants with a portion of his riches. The wise servants use what they have to grow the riches, but the lazy servant does nothing with what he's been given. When the master returns, each servant gives an account of how he's used his gifts for the master's benefit.

God has given each of us gifts to use for His glory. To some, He's given speaking abilities or artistic talent or a magnetic personality. Others might have material wealth to provide for the needs of others. It doesn't matter what the gift is, if we aren't using it for God's glory, we might as well bury it in the ground.

In the end, we'll have to answer our Master for how we've used His gifts. Will He say well done?

Lord, help me use my gifts, talents, and abilities for Your glory instead of burying them in my selfish ambitions.

THE WAY OF PERSONAL PAIN

Fools because of their transgression,
and because of their iniquities, are afflicted.
PSALM 107:17

Foolishness and trouble are cause-and-effect companions. The cause is foolishness, and the effect is trouble. No one wants trouble to show up, but foolishness opens the door to its entry.

A fool isn't interested in the truth. He is prone to rebellion and likes to wander a path of his own choosing. That path often has spiritual thistles, unseen drop-offs, and multiple tripping hazards. Yet time and again a fool will smile and choose the way of personal pain, thinking it will be different this time. But it never is. It isn't now. It never will be.

The good news is that you do not have to choose the path fools take. That path is an option worth rejection for no other reason than it has proved a failed option.

Let's turn that around. A wise person refuses rebellion—and, while he may suffer as much as anyone else, the suffering he experiences will not be due to his own rebellious choices.

Set aside personal rebellion, and things will begin to improve. It will mean a change of heart, thinking, and the way to respond to God.

God, I don't need to have a testimony of foolishness to tell others about You. I don't need to keep being foolish. Help me to believe that and make wise decisions.

LOOKING INSIDE

The LORD said unto Samuel, Look not on his countenance, or on the height of his stature; because I have refused him: for the LORD seeth not as man seeth; for man looketh on the outward appearance, but the LORD looketh on the heart.

1 SAMUEL 16:7

The prophet Samuel had a job: God told him to find the second king of Israel. The search narrowed to the sons of Jesse. Samuel spent time with each of seven, some of whom were quite impressive—but God said no to each. So Samuel asked Jesse if there were any others. As it turns out there was one more. . .but from Jesse's perspective this boy didn't really count. David was out watching over flocks of sheep. It seems it never even entered Jesse's mind to ask David to come in from his work detail.

When Samuel met David he knew that this young man would be Israel's next king. How? Well, God told him, of course. The Lord informed His prophet that he shouldn't always believe his eyes. Samuel needed to trust God, who saw more in David than a mere shepherd boy.

God's wisdom looks at what a man is on the inside. This wisdom isn't about popularity or who has the most money. God's wisdom sees the potential that He has placed inside a person.

Lord, remind me to ask You every time I have a decision to make. Please guide me into Your wise ways.

DON'T FEAR

Fear none of those things which thou shalt suffer: behold, the devil shall cast some of you into prison, that ye may be tried; and ye shall have tribulation ten days: be thou faithful unto death, and I will give thee a crown of life.

Revelation 2:10

Throughout church history, Christians have expected to suffer for the cause of Christ. The New Testament is full of such understanding. First Peter 4:13 says, "But rejoice, inasmuch as ye are partakers of Christ's sufferings; that, when his glory shall be revealed, ye may be glad also with exceeding joy." Romans 8:17–18 says, "And if children, then heirs; heirs of God, and joint-heirs with Christ; if so be that we suffer with him, that we may be also glorified together. For I reckon that the sufferings of this present time are not worthy to be compared with the glory which shall be revealed in us." (See also 2 Corinthians 4:17; James 1:2–3; and 2 Timothy 2:12.)

Today's verse says we should not fear suffering for the name of Jesus, but rather, be faithful unto death. You will be here one moment and with the Lord the next (2 Corinthians 5:8). Whatever consequences you face today for your faith in Christ, do so knowing it will all be worth it.

Lord, help me not to fear suffering here on earth, for I know that by remaining faithful to death, I will receive the crown of life.

DISREGARDING INSTRUCTIONS

All we like sheep have gone astray;
we have turned every one to his own way.
ISAIAH 53:6

You don't follow directions as well as you should. No one does. You go to the store with your wife's approved list of necessities and bring home something only a guy would enjoy. You're given directions to a specific location and you explore a shortcut. You're given a set of instructions for a piece of furniture but have parts left over when the project is done. Of course, you disregarded the instructions, but claimed there was a manufacturer's error.

Here are two realities: The first is that God provided life instructions. The second is that men often consider these instructions as suggestions that can be altered at will.

If God tells you to go north, you might think it's better to go south. . .since north sounds cold. If God instructs you to share you might choose to keep, because a time may come when you need that stuff. If God instructs you to love you might choose to withhold love, because love leaves no room for revenge.

And like sheep outside the view of the shepherd you wander around with no idea of where you are or how you got there. By disregarding God's wisdom you *will* go astray.

Help me to recognize when I'm disregarding Your instructions, Lord. May I walk with You and resist every urge to wander away from Your wisdom.

MORE THAN A PERSONAL PURSUIT

To the intent that now unto the principalities and powers in heavenly places might be known by the church the manifold wisdom of God, according to the eternal purpose which he purposed in Christ Jesus our Lord.
EPHESIANS 3:10–11

Seeking godly wisdom for yourself is just the start of what God wants. He wants wisdom to be a global pursuit, yet each day you'll make foolish choices or see them being made by others. God wants His wisdom known and celebrated by His people. He's not content with just your personal pursuit of wisdom. He wants it shared, for other people to be inspired to begin their own individual journeys to wisdom.

When wisdom is known, people begin to understand the value of the body of Christ. You're salt. You're light. You're a representative of the wisdom of God that brings civil actions to civilization. There's never a good reason to keep wisdom hidden.

Use wisdom to direct personal actions, but also use wisdom to open doors to a collective movement among those you know. When others understand the importance of God, society can chart a renewed course with an improved outcome.

Seek to know the difference, share the difference, be the difference.

May my pursuit encourage a movement toward wisdom, Lord. May others see the value, share the experience, and refuse to keep wisdom to themselves.

THE EYE TEST

I will set no wicked thing before mine eyes: I hate the work of them that turn aside; it shall not cleave to me.

Psalm 101:3

The eyes, it is said, are the window to the soul. What we look at not only affects our souls but also reveals our souls. It's so important for us as Christian men to be careful with what we place within our vision.

David, the writer of Psalm 101, knew this. And isn't it interesting that he was thinking about this a thousand years before Christ? It would be naive to think that the ancients didn't have visual temptations in their lives. What were they? There were no illicit magazines, movies, or TV shows that streamed spiritual death into their homes. These people couldn't access all manner of unspeakable depravity with a click of their phones or laptops.

Yet somehow, in some way, there were temptations. So David vowed to the Lord not to set evil before his eyes.

Every Christian man in the twenty-first century—amid the innumerable temptations we face—should keep the same vow to God. We should have nothing to do with pornography and inappropriate sexual content in any other media. Like Joseph did when Potiphar's wife made advances, we should turn and run.

Let's make a wise vow to the Lord to honor Him and others with our eyes.

God, I want to honor You. Give me the strength to set nothing wicked before my eyes.

PRECIOUS, BLESSED MEMORIES

Only take heed to thyself, and keep thy soul diligently, lest thou forget the things which thine eyes have seen, and lest they depart from thy heart all the days of thy life: but teach them thy sons, and thy sons' sons.
DEUTERONOMY 4:9

Human beings tend to treasure certain types of memories: weddings, the births of children, graduations, sports achievements—the list goes on and on. Opening up scrapbooks, watching videos, or just discussing pleasant memories are wonderful ways to spend an evening. They can certainly strengthen bonds of family and friendship.

It's good to do the same thing with your Father in heaven. In several passages of scripture (including the verse above), God encourages His people to remember the amazing things He has done for them.

Today, make some time to remember God's goodness to you in the past. Think about the moment He saved you and made you part of His eternal family—and about how He's helped you to grow into the man of God you are today. Remember the times He helped you out of a terrible jam or gave you wisdom about a certain situation. And consider those amazing instances when it was obvious that He had moved on your behalf as a direct result of prayer.

Father, help me to remember Your goodness to me so that my faith in and love for You may remain strong and growing.

WISDOM IS FAIR

Ye shall do no unrighteousness in judgment: thou shalt not respect the person of the poor, nor honor the person of the mighty: but in righteousness shalt thou judge thy neighbour.
LEVITICUS 19:15

Every day we contemplate what's fair. It might seem as if someone who's poor can be excused from a crime because he had faced hard circumstances. We might also assume that a rich person is guilty because we consider the wealthy to be greedy. But today's scripture from Leviticus, God's lawbook, indicates that neither idea represents the fairness God wants His family to embrace.

You're not to consider those with less financial means as beneath you or above the law. You're not to consider those with more financial means as above you or free to do whatever they please.

God looks at the heart of every individual, determining the true motivation for his every action. And the Lord tells us to consider facts and leave assumptions alone. If you don't know the truth then at the very least stop talking about it as if you do.

Wisdom recognizes that God is impartial. And He wants you to also be impartial in dealing with the people He made.

Lord, I can be quick to judge without having all the facts You possess. But I know Your wisdom is fair. Please help me to simply love people and allow You to lead them in a better direction.

EDIFY ONE ANOTHER

Let us therefore follow after the things which make for peace, and things wherewith one may edify another.
Romans 14:19

In this portion of scripture, Paul urges Christians from different backgrounds to set aside their disagreements about clean or unclean food. He calls such notions a "stumblingblock," an "occasion to fall in his brother's way" (Romans 14:13). All in all, these disagreements are hindrances to growth in faith: "For the kingdom of God is not meat and drink; but righteousness, and peace, and joy in the Holy Ghost" (verse 17). Notice that the call in today's verse isn't to be "right" about such things but, rather, to make peace and to edify one another.

Your Christian friends might not argue over what foods to eat, but perhaps they take different stances on alcohol usage, spiritual gifts, worship styles, the end times, church governance, or other topics. Talking through such matters will be edifying, if it's done in the right spirit. But why not focus more on wise, Christian living for the mutual benefit of all involved?

You could steer the conversation toward concepts such as loving God and neighbor, practicing forgiveness, ways to serve others, evangelism, striving for personal holiness, ways to practice gratitude, resisting temptation, practicing self-control, how to be a good steward of time and money and talents. . .among many others.

Lord, make me an instrument of peace in my Christian circles so that we can edify one another.

COLLECTIVE WISDOM

Keep therefore and do them; for this is your wisdom and your understanding in the sight of the nations, which shall hear all these statutes, and say, Surely this great nation is a wise and understanding people.
DEUTERONOMY 4:6

God had given His people laws. They were clear and concise. They were birthed in the heart of God, and the people were to do what God wanted them to do. If the people would universally follow God, this would display wisdom and understanding for every other nation to observe. Their collective willingness to obey would allow them to introduce their God to those nations that would ask, "Why do you live differently?"

God indicated in Deuteronomy 4 that other nations would respect a nation that was wise enough to follow—because God was doing the leading. Wise enough to obey, when others struggled to do so. Wise enough to acknowledge God, when others assumed He was a myth.

We're all human, and human beings break God's laws. Society continues to look for collective wisdom in a people. Let's commit ourselves, as the church of Jesus Christ, to show them.

I want to be wise by following You, God. Please help me and my spiritual brothers and sisters to do that consistently, today and every day.

LOVE. . .YOUR ENEMIES?

Ye have heard that it hath been said, Thou shalt love thy neighbour, and hate thine enemy. But I say unto you, Love your enemies, bless them that curse you, do good to them that hate you, and pray for them which despitefully use you, and persecute you; that ye may be the children of your Father which is in heaven: for he maketh his sun to rise on the evil and on the good, and sendeth rain on the just and on the unjust.

MATTHEW 5:43–45

Some people are just fundamentally unpleasant. They are rude, demanding, churlish, selfish, and unkind—and that's on their good days! Still others, through no fault of yours, just don't like you. They'll speak ill of you and treat you as an enemy.

In the passage above, Jesus offers some heavenly wisdom for dealing with people who, for whatever reason, view you as a foe: Love them anyway, in both word and deed.

How we treat the unlovable, Jesus taught, reflects our relationship with our heavenly Father. It shows we understand that we are also sinners, just saved by God's grace. We've all been selfish. We've all hurt and offended others.

Yet God chooses to love us—so much so that while we were still sinners, He sent Jesus to die for us. Now we are called to pass the love along.

Lord Jesus, some people are not easy to love. But I want to be like You and love them anyway. Give me the wisdom and will to obey Your command to love my enemies.

THE HYPOCRISY DILEMMA

Both prophet and priest are profane; yea, in my house have I found their wickedness, saith the LORD.
JEREMIAH 23:11

A good lesson in wisdom is to admit that no human being is perfect. God pointed out this fact to the prophet Jeremiah. The Lord shone a spotlight on the wickedness of hypocrisy among those who served Him in the temple.

This shouldn't come as a surprise. If the people who serve in any church are human (and they are) then there will be individuals who sin within the walls of the church. The Bible is clear that all people sin—so there will always be hypocrisy in any place where humans get together. That includes the government, the news media, the educational establishment. . .and the church.

It's wise to acknowledge that hypocrisy exists. And it's wise to recognize that God uses broken people to be His hands and feet in a society that needs to know Him. You might resist going to church because of the hypocrites there, but you'll face pretenders everywhere you go.

By attending a true house of worship, we admit we want to do something about the pretending. Let's commit to banishing hypocrisy from our own hearts, and then to sharing an honest vision of Jesus Christ with everyone we meet.

I need to remember that forgiveness is needed even in church, God. Your love doesn't stop because a person has messed up again. Remind me that You are working in lives everywhere, both inside and outside of Your church.

HUMILITY IS WISDOM

John answered them, saying, I baptize with water: but there standeth one among you, whom ye know not; he it is, who coming after me is preferred before me, whose shoe's latchet I am not worthy to unloose.
JOHN 1:26–27

Do you remember how Jesus viewed His relative and forerunner John? The Lord said, "Among them that are born of women there hath not risen a greater than John the Baptist" (Matthew 11:11). Yet in today's scripture, see how John judged himself: The pinnacle of "them that are born of women" said he wasn't worthy of untying Jesus' shoes.

That's the attitude God wants in His children. "By humility and the fear of the LORD are riches, and honour, and life," Proverbs 22:4 says. "With the lowly is wisdom," Proverbs 11:2 adds, and "before honour is humility" (Proverbs 18:12). "Let nothing be done through strife or vainglory," the apostle Paul taught, "but in lowliness of mind let each esteem other better than themselves" (Philippians 2:3). Encapsulating all, famed Bible teacher Oswald Chambers said, "Humility is the one stamp of a saint."

No matter how impressive you are, someone is always more so. And even if you happen to be this generation's John the Baptist, you're still unworthy of loosening Jesus' sandals. That's just fine. Remember, if we don't come to Jesus as little children, we don't get into His kingdom (Matthew 18:3).

Lord Jesus, my life is all about You. May I always view myself with appropriate humility.

INITIALLY SCOFFED

I believed not the words, until I came, and mine eyes had seen it: and, behold, the half was not told me: thy wisdom and prosperity exceedeth the fame which I heard.

1 Kings 10:7

The Queen of Sheba had heard what she likely considered a legend: King Solomon's wisdom was said to be superior to all other men. She probably thought he was knowledgeable, but the stories she'd heard must have been exaggerated. But this queen decided it was worth her time to see and hear for herself. She made her travel plans and went to meet this legendary king. And she was so impressed that she claimed all the things she'd heard didn't describe Solomon half as well as they should have.

It's safe to say that wise people are often scoffed at initially. Why? Well, wise people often go against popular opinion. They make decisions that don't take into account poll numbers and popularity contests. They may even seem foolish—until their choices and thoughts are proven true, reliable, and helpful.

Wisdom may not always make you popular or famous. But wise people will always be remembered for their belief in truth and their trust in God's good outcome.

I want to be brave enough to pursue wisdom, Father. Help me to be strong enough to seek Your answers and then to do the things I'm learning from You.

PUTTING SELF LAST

And he sat down, and called the twelve,
and saith unto them, If any man desire to be first,
the same shall be last of all, and servant of all.
MARK 9:35

Jesus knew that His disciples had been arguing among themselves—they'd been discussing which of them was the most important. It was time for some wise kingdom teaching.

The Lord knew exactly what was going on, but still He asked the men, "What was it that ye disputed among yourselves by the way?" (Mark 9:33). Hearing no answer, Jesus sat them down and said, "If anyone wants to be first, he must be last of all and servant of all."

That teaching that day still holds true for Christian men today. Jesus calls each of us to, as Paul wrote, "esteem other better than themselves" (Philippians 2:3).

Being "last of all" and a "servant of all" doesn't mean you aren't important or useful to God. It doesn't mean you're to engage in phony self-effacement. It simply means that you consistently treat others like they are more important than you are. It means serving in any way you can and sharing what you have with people in need.

Do you want to be great in God's kingdom? Then make it your goal to serve others in humility and put others ahead of yourself.

Lord Jesus, give me the wisdom to remember that You want me to put others ahead of myself, to care for others every day.

REMAIN TEACHABLE

Better is a poor and a wise child than an old and foolish king, who will no more be admonished.
ECCLESIASTES 4:13

Have you ever been around people who can't be informed—because they already know everything? If you mention a topic they'll choose the role of expert, even if they must make up what they're saying.

God found it important to say that a child who chooses wisdom is better than a king who refuses advice. This would be the contrast between someone who listens before making decisions and one who only wants others to agree with them—even when wrong.

Wisdom knows more than anyone else in the room, but it remains teachable. Foolishness doesn't need facts to form an opinion—and it will share its opinion with everyone nearby.

This kind of foolish speaking doesn't need to be true—it only needs an audience. Wisdom can speak truth even when no one's willing to listen.

You may be young or more mature. Foolishness and wisdom will always seek to gain your attention. Which will you accept?

Lord God, please help me to see wisdom as something worth pursuing, exploring, and sharing. I want to remove the welcome mat when foolishness drops by.

TRUST IS WISDOM

Some trust in chariots, and some in horses: but we will remember the name of the LORD our God.
PSALM 20:7

Chariots were the M1 Abrams tanks of the ancient world. For power, speed, and instilling fear in an enemy, few weapons on the battlefield rivaled an armada of fierce chariots kicking up a massive cloud of dust as they sped toward the front lines.

Some of the most powerful empires of antiquity—the Hittites, Egyptians, Assyrians, Babylonians, Greeks, and Chinese—employed chariots to great effect. Yet in Deuteronomy 17:16, God forbade Israel from amassing large amounts of horses, obviously a necessity for chariot warfare.

Why? Was God setting Israel up to fail? No, He was setting them up to trust.

In Deuteronomy 20:1, God told Israel, "When thou goest out to battle against thine enemies, and seest horses, and chariots, and a people more than thou, be not afraid of them: for the LORD thy God is with thee."

Clearly, chariots are a thing of the past. But today we can divert our trust into plenty of other options: bank accounts, retirement funds, good education, a plum job, home security systems, family members, doctors, church leaders, a political party or candidate . . . the list goes on.

God calls us to something far better: He calls us to trust in Him. This is true wisdom.

God, in all aspects of my life, help me to trust in You and You alone.

THINK BEFORE YOU SPEAK

And the men of Israel were distressed that day: for Saul had adjured the people, saying, Cursed be the man that eateth any food until evening, that I may be avenged on mine enemies. So none of the people tasted any food.

1 Samuel 14:24

Just imagine the trouble we'd avoid if we all took the advice of today's devotional title. Individually, culturally, worldwide—how helpful to recognize the truth of Proverbs 13:3: "He that keepeth his mouth keepeth his life: but he that openeth wide his lips shall have destruction."

King Saul spoke rashly when he pronounced a curse on any soldier who ate before nightfall. Israel's troops could have enjoyed the refreshment of plentiful honey they found in the woods, "but no man put his hand to his mouth: for the people feared the oath" (1 Samuel 14:26). Jonathan, the king's son who'd been out successfully fighting Philistines when Saul issued his foolish order, *did* eat some honey, and his eyes were "enlightened" (verse 29). He recognized that the soldiers would have been more effective with food in their stomachs.

Saul's order resulted in a death penalty on Jonathan, and the mass disobedience of the rest of the army to save the young man's life. How unnecessary it all was.

Today, let's commit ourselves to James' wisdom: "Let every man be swift to hear, slow to speak, slow to wrath" (1:19).

Lord, may my thoughts be many and my words few.

BETTER THAN AN ACTION HERO

Wisdom strengtheneth the wise more than ten mighty men which are in the city.
Ecclesiastes 7:19

Using the remote to access an action-adventure flick is a way some men choose to unwind. If you've ever done that, keep in mind the picture of a hero who seems capable of taking on an army all by himself and emerging victorious. There's not a lot of talking in these movies—they're all about brute force and a few quotable phrases.

King Solomon wrote a script including ten mighty action-adventure heroes—"mighty men"—contrasting them with wisdom. His conclusion was that wisdom made one man stronger than ten mighty heroes.

This is a bold statement in a world that exalts physically strong men. Wise men will always work smarter—not harder. They can dispel volatile discussions with calm assurance. They can turn the tide on violent encounters. When people are wise they're much greater heroes than anyone who resorts to physical strength to solve issues.

You can be both physically strong and intentionally wise. Be a hero who uses wise words from a wise heart inspired by a wise God.

Lord, let me rely on Your wisdom more than my own ability to manage daily struggles. I want to see wisdom transform difficult situations that I could never control on my own.

DEFUSE

A soft answer turneth away wrath: but grievous words stir up anger.
Proverbs 15:1

Knock-down, drag-out arguments are glorified on TV. Think of the last action or drama you watched. The detective and the police chief who can't see eye to eye. The husband and wife on opposite sides of an issue. The estranged father and son. Many shows end in explosive shouting matches until, somehow, someone makes a point that silences the other person. They've won. The credits roll.

That may work on television, but the Bible presents wisdom for real life. Here, in this world, when two people continue to incite each other's anger, it rarely ends in understanding. Shouting matches only make things worse. Words are said that cannot be unsaid. Doors get slammed. Holes get kicked in the drywall.

Fortunately, God has equipped you to soothe anger. It's not by shouting people down or putting them in their place. The most effective way to speak to an angry person is with soft words. Grace. Understanding. Cool-headedness.

Soft answers defuse arguments before they can explode. Even when you are angry, use what you can control—your words. Master the art of speaking soft answers. This is the path of wisdom.

Lord, I want the wisdom required to defuse angry situations. Please help me to speak soft answers.

BEWARE THE PROSPERITY TRAP

Moreover all these curses shall come upon thee, and shall pursue thee, and overtake thee, till thou be destroyed; because thou hearkenedst not unto the voice of the LORD thy God, to keep his commandments and his statutes which he commanded thee: and they shall be upon thee for a sign and for a wonder, and upon thy seed for ever. Because thou servedst not the LORD thy God with joyfulness, and with gladness of heart, for the abundance of all things.

DEUTERONOMY 28:45–47

God had called the people of Israel to be a sign to all nations of His power and glory. If the people abandoned that sacred mission, their future would darken. The greatest threat to their future was, in fact, their prosperity, which could cause them to forget their need for God.

You or someone you know may be praying for God's provision right now. While such prayers are encouraged and modeled throughout the Bible, there is a dark side. As you depend on God for your provision, the comfort and prosperity He sends can affect your mindset. You might start depending on your own resources and wisdom. You can lose sight of your need for God and assume your own wisdom led to your success. Be sure you avoid that trap.

Wealth isn't necessarily a blessing unless you continue to joyfully serve God.

Lord, help me to joyfully serve You in faith and hope without being distracted by what I have.

THINGS HE COULDN'T FIX

For in much wisdom is much grief: and he that increaseth knowledge increaseth sorrow.
ECCLESIASTES 1:18

The title of "wisest man on earth" was indisputably King Solomon's. Yet, as he aged, Solomon wrote of a certain weight that comes with wisdom. It may seem strange, but the more Solomon understood the more he recognized things like the breaking of God's law, the breaking of the human heart, and the breaking of trust between humans.

As wise as Solomon was, there were just certain things he couldn't fix. He understood so many of the things mankind thinks and the intentions of the heart. Many weren't noble or wise. Solomon even knew that wisdom wasn't a gift that he could pass on to his children. Each would have to decide to pursue wisdom on their own. They could also refuse to pursue it—and many would.

This caused sorrow for a man who knew how to make things better. . .but couldn't force others to understand their need of wisdom.

You also have the choice to pursue wisdom or not. How will you respond today?

Lord, I can't rely on anyone else's wisdom—my parents', my friends', my pastor's. I'm asking to be wise for myself, with the wisdom only You can provide.

DO GOOD

*But to do good and to communicate forget not:
for with such sacrifices God is well pleased.*
HEBREWS 13:16

Most people spend the majority of their day thinking about themselves. That's been confirmed by several studies. One found that seventy-eight percent of conversations involved talking about ourselves and our perceptions of the world. Another one documents that thirty to forty percent of everyday speech is used to relay information to others about one's own experiences or personal relationships. And yet another study indicates that upward of eighty percent of social media posts consist of announcements about one's own experiences.

The author of Hebrews calls Christians to a different standard. Rather than thinking constantly about our own interests, we are to think about the poor and needy, as Galatians 6:10 reminds us: "As we have therefore opportunity, let us do good unto all men, especially unto them who are of the household of faith." And we are to stir one another up to do the same—"to communicate forget not"—which means to share what you have.

We do these things because God has done the same for us. Now it pleases Him when we do good in His name for others.

Lord, I want to think about people in need—especially those who are of the household of faith—far more than I think about myself. Remind me to do so today.

IMAGINE A WORLD

Thou shalt not avenge, nor bear any grudge against the children of thy people, but thou shalt love thy neighbour as thyself: I am the LORD.

LEVITICUS 19:18

Imagine a world like the one described in Leviticus 19. It would be a place without grudges and nosey neighbors. There would be no GET OFF MY LAWN signs or plots of revenge. Gone would be the recollection of an unreturned tool or offensive act. It would be a world where sharing was common. If something was broken or lost it would never separate friends. People would look out for others, and no one would try to get anyone else in trouble.

In this world people wouldn't try to prove they were superior to anyone else. There would be no prejudice or class systems. There would be ongoing moments of care. Locked doors would be unnecessary.

It is wise to embrace this view—if not for the entire world, certainly for within God's church. Unless and until God chooses to save a majority of our fellow human beings, trouble will continue in the larger world. But we as Christian brothers and sisters have every reason and resource to do what Leviticus 19:18 says. Today, let's commit to doing that.

Lord God, You want Your people especially to get along, to forgive each other, and to love with great compassion. As much as it depends on me, help me to live this way.

HEAVENLY THOUGHTS

Set your affection on things above, not on things on the earth.
COLOSSIANS 3:2

You may have heard someone say a Christian can be so heavenly minded that he's no earthly good. But C. S. Lewis would have disagreed with that. In *Mere Christianity*, he wrote, "A continual looking forward to the eternal world is not (as some modern people think) a form of escapism or wishful thinking, but one of the things a Christian is meant to do. It does not mean that we are to leave the present world as it is. If you read history you will find that the Christians who did most for the present world were just those who thought most of the next."

In what ways might you think the most of the next world—that is, heaven? It starts with our thought life, as Philippians 4:8 suggests: "Finally, brethren, whatsoever things are true, whatsoever things are honest, whatsoever things are just, whatsoever things are pure, whatsoever things are lovely, whatsoever things are of good report; if there be any virtue, and if there be any praise, think on these things." Elsewhere, the apostle Paul said it this way: "For to be carnally minded is death; but to be spiritually minded is life and peace" (Romans 8:6).

Lord God, I want to set my affection on things above—on things that matter for all eternity. Give me the wisdom I need to think heavenly thoughts today.

WORK AS WISDOM

For what hath man of all his labour, and of the vexation of his heart, wherein he hath laboured under the sun? For all his days are sorrows, and his travail grief; yea, his heart taketh not rest in the night. This is also vanity. There is nothing better for a man, than that he should eat and drink, and that he should make his soul enjoy good in his labour. This also I saw, that it was from the hand of God.

ECCLESIASTES 2:22–24

Work is a useful tool in developing wisdom. For many, it can seem a drudgery and struggle that should be endured—or avoided. But for those who follow Christ, the idea of work as an element of wisdom is shown in using what you earn to provide for your own family and then for people in need. It's a chance to develop skills that God has given you to impact the lives of other people.

There's satisfaction in work that has meaning for a man himself and a benefit for society. The struggle happens when we refuse to consider the needs of others, when we don't look for opportunities to help. Wisdom says, "There is nothing better for a man, than that he should eat and drink, and that he should make his soul enjoy good in his labour." This is from the hand of God.

Thank You for the concept of work, Lord. Let it remind me that You continue to work on me. Please help me see work as an opportunity to serve You and help others.

YOUR MAIN FOCUS

But seek ye first the kingdom of God, and his righteousness; and all these things shall be added unto you.
MATTHEW 6:33

Have you ever generated a prayer list of your responsibilities as a man, a husband, a father, and an employee or business owner? Every man has any number of important responsibilities on earth—responsibilities that, if not met, greatly impact others in our lives, including those we love most dearly.

It's not wrong for you to think about caring for yourself, your family, and others you love. In fact, God calls you to do just that. He put these people in your life and He wants you to protect and provide for them.

But these responsibilities, important as they are, should not be your life's top priority.

God wants you to put *all things*—even your wife and children—behind your relationship with Him. Don't let anything, even your most pressing needs and responsibilities, take your focus off the God who loves you so much that He sent Jesus to die for you. Putting the Lord and His kingdom first is wisdom, and He will take care of everything else.

Jesus, You have promised that our Father in heaven will give me everything I need to live my life on earth. Help me to focus on You and Your kingdom above all other things.

UNDERSTAND GOD'S LOVINGKINDNESS

Whoso is wise, and will observe these things, even they shall understand the lovingkindness of the LORD.

PSALM 107:43

Psalm 107, which appears to have been written after the Jews returned to the Promised Land following the Babylonian exile, describes four groups of people whom God rescued.

The first group includes those people who "wandered in the wilderness in a solitary way" (Psalm 107:4). The second group includes those who "sit in darkness and in the shadow of death, being bound in affliction and iron" (verse 10). The third group includes "fools because of their transgression, and because of their iniquities, are afflicted" (verse 17). The fourth group includes those "that go down to the sea in ships" (verse 23).

Each of these groups of people, whether of their own making or not, faced trouble and danger. And what was the fate of each? The Lord redeemed and gathered them. In every specific situation, God extended His love and saved them.

No matter what serious trouble you face in life, God is present in your situation. He has always saved His people and always will. So "observe these things" and "understand the lovingkindness of the LORD."

God, You have helped me so many times in the past. Now, as I face new challenges, help me to remember Your lovingkindness.

WISDOM ALWAYS WANTS TRUTH

Beware lest any man spoil you through philosophy and vain deceit, after the tradition of men, after the rudiments of the world, and not after Christ.

COLOSSIANS 2:8

Wisdom makes you less gullible. People can say some very interesting things—and they sound convincing. You can apply their words to what you know about God and come away with something that God never said. In fact, you might believe things that violate other things He clearly said in His Word.

In the Bible these kinds of people were called false prophets. They looked and sounded the part, but their words contained none of the wisdom of God. You could always tell a false prophet because what they said never came true. They shared messages that God didn't send.

Most people don't have time to wait to see the bad fruit of lying lips. That's why wisdom is important. Getting closer to God's truth through the wisdom He offers will help you recognize what is false. Then you can get closer to the things that are true and worthwhile.

People are really good at rewriting truth to conform to their own desires, to describe a world they wish was true—but that's called *fiction*. Wisdom will always want to discover the truth.

I want to learn from You, Lord. I want to be the type of man who recognizes the many shades of fiction I'll encounter—and trust You to teach me truth.

PEACE BEFORE WAR

The work of righteousness shall be peace; and the effect of righteousness quietness and assurance for ever.
Isaiah 32:17

Have you ever been "triggered"? It's a common affliction. Someone says something you think was intended to make you mad. It can seem like certain folks are looking for opportunities to bring out your worst. Sometimes you go along with them.

Wisdom says you don't allow these triggers to throw your environment into chaos. You measure your reply carefully when someone is trying to upset you. In fact, your response is one of the few things you can control in these situations.

When you're given a big bag of discontentment seeds, you can always refuse to plant them. You sure don't need to nurture them. You don't need to keep checking for their first blooms. Saying no to the reactionary life will help your own mental, physical, and spiritual well-being, and it will honor your Lord.

Wisdom is always found in seeking peace before welcoming war.

Lord God, the less-than-kind words of others can make my emotions boil. Please give me the wisdom to think, reflect, and pray before I say or do things I regret.

TURNING THE OTHER CHEEK

To speak evil of no man, to be no brawlers,
but gentle, shewing all meekness unto all men.
TITUS 3:2

Way back in 1996, NBA power forward A. C. Green was elbowed in the mouth during a game. Green lost his two front teeth, and even the sockets that held them were cracked. "For most people, the instinct would be to fight back," said an Associated Press story. "Not Green. He picked up his teeth and left the court." Charles Barkley, who was Green's teammate on the Phoenix Suns at the time, told him, "Now I know you're a real Christian."

The apostle Paul's call to Titus in today's verse is one of meekness toward all men. Christians should not be given to brawling, but show gentleness and humility at all times.

What is your first instinct when you're punched in the mouth, literally or figuratively? The Bible allows for self-defense (Exodus 22:2–3), but the greater call for the believer is one of self-*control*—a non-retaliatory response. You can show unbelievers the truth of the gospel by turning the other cheek. It might just prove to them that Christianity is real.

Lord, please make my response to aggression wise—not brawling, but gentle, showing meekness to all men.

ENQUIRING MINDS

David enquired of God.
1 CHRONICLES 14:10

There's more to this passage than "David enquired." It was a mix of strategy and military action. It was a desire to win. Yes, there's more to the story, yet four words make this story more than an impulse decision: "David enquired of God."

This king had fought and won wars, but he had also written psalms, hymns, and spiritual songs. He had a close relationship with God, and leaving Him out of this story made no sense to David. Instead of guessing, David enquired. Instead of assuming, David enquired. Instead of ignoring, David enquired.

It's easy to leave someone out of a decision, especially when you think that person might disagree with what you want to do. We like to find people who agree with us, even when we think we might be wrong. But that's a foolish way to address life's tough issues.

Bring God into your plans, and allow Him to veto what He knows is a waste of your time and energy. Give Him every chance possible to answer your enquiry.

Father, please help me to ask for Your answers to the questions that are too hard for me. Then give me the wisdom to listen to Your direction and pursue it.

WISDOM IN GIVING UP?

They that wait upon the LORD *shall renew their strength; they shall mount up with wings as eagles; they shall run, and not be weary; and they shall walk, and not faint.*

ISAIAH 40:31

If you think there's wisdom in giving up, it depends on *what* you're giving up.

Depression is a real and present condition that can be debilitating. People often look at life wondering if it's time to simply give up. It's not. The circumstances around you aren't greater than the God at work in you. He hasn't given up on you. He uses His mercy and grace to offer hope to those who've come to believe such hope is the stuff of fables.

Letting go of all that you think and feel is the proper way of giving up. Wisdom is paying attention to what God says, not simply how you're feeling.

Life is a journey and you'll need help to run and walk without weariness of mind and body. The strength you need is the strength God offers. The hope you need will be found in Him. The joy that you need is found in the wisdom of knowing He's always in control.

Heavenly Father, I'd like to run, but sometimes my circumstances leave me crawling. I ask for Your strength so I can run, walk, and soar.

KNOW GOD

And thou, Solomon my son, know thou the God of thy father, and serve him with a perfect heart and with a willing mind: for the LORD searcheth all hearts, and understandeth all the imaginations of the thoughts: if thou seek him, he will be found of thee; but if thou forsake him, he will cast thee off for ever.

1 CHRONICLES 28:9

It was time for King David to pass the kingdom to his son Solomon. This father's wisdom for the incoming king is good wisdom for you: Know, understand, appreciate, obey, and cherish God. Serve Him with a heart that refuses rebellion and a mind that is ready for a God adventure. He can and will search the core of who you are, and He is fully aware of your tendency to wander. Seek God, pray to Him, learn from Him. Make that your primary goal, and you will find Him.

That's an amazing bit of advice. It encourages every part of you to enlist in a lifetime of learning, a heart of wisdom, and a spirit that recognizes the goodness of God.

Heavenly Father, help me take David's advice and gain wisdom. May Your wisdom change my heart for the better.

WISE TO MEMORIZE

Thy word have I hid in mine heart, that I might not sin against thee.
Psalm 119:11

Memorization is a big part of the human experience. From the beginning moments of school, we memorized our ABCs and 1-2-3s. Later, we memorized facts about the human body, historical events, the stars and planets, and mathematical and scientific realities. At work and at home, we memorize way too many computer passwords. In marriage, we memorize birthdays and anniversaries. . .at least, we'd better!

But how much time do we commit to memorizing scripture?

The author of Psalm 119—writing before the Old Testament canon was finished and without the benefit of the New Testament—understood the importance of memorizing God's Word. Do we?

Committing scripture to memory helps us in all phases of life. Having God's Word at the ready guides our thoughts, decisions, conversations, relationships, prayer life, and so much more. God's Word tells us who we are, who God is, and what He expects of us. It reveals the glorious realities of the gospel of Jesus Christ, both for the present and on into eternity. It keeps us on the path of righteousness, convicts us of sin, and reminds us of God's steadfast love and grace.

Those who are wise hide God's Word in their hearts.

Lord, thank You for Your Word. Help me to hide it in my heart that I might not sin against You.

WHAT DO YOU TREASURE?

My son, keep my words, and lay up my commandments with thee. Keep my commandments, and live; and my law as the apple of thine eye. Bind them upon thy fingers, write them upon the table of thine heart. Say unto wisdom, Thou art my sister; and call understanding thy kinswoman.

Proverbs 7:1–4

The things you treasure and store up in your heart will eventually determine the way you live.

There is plenty we can think about and treasure besides the ways of God. That's often where our troubles begin. What is at the forefront of your mind right now? Is it God's wisdom and commands, or are your thoughts directed by the worries of life, entertainment, or some lofty goals you've set for yourself? The voices on your TV, radio, or phone can drown out the still, small voice of God's Spirit calling out to you.

Consider how you can treasure God's words today. You may need more silence to be attentive to Him. You may need more time to ponder the words of scripture. Perhaps you should start with removing the distractions, misplaced priorities, and white noise that makes it tough to notice God in the first place.

Lord, please help me to remove the distractions that keep me from treasuring Your commandments in my heart. May Your wisdom guide my steps.

WISDOM OF THE ELDERS

Holding fast the faithful word as he hath been taught, that he may be able by sound doctrine both to exhort and to convince the gainsayers.

Titus 1:9

Today's verse describes an appointed elder of the church. It gives guidelines on whom to look for when choosing someone to help lead God's people.

But these qualifications aren't just limited to elders; they're applicable to any Christian man who desires a closer walk with God. So when you read today's verse, ask yourself, *Do I have these qualities? Is my faith strong enough to weather the doubts that the world throws my way? Do I encourage others or disappoint them? Am I able to discern between truth and error?*

Nobody wakes up one morning with all of these qualities in their lives. It takes a lifetime of honing your spiritual skills, digging deeply into God's Word and regularly seeking His will, to reach this place. That's why the leaders in question are known as "elders"—they've lived their lives seeking godliness and slowly acquiring wisdom.

So in your quest to become like them, don't be afraid to learn from them. Find Christians who embody these traits, ask them questions, and remember their example each time you face hard decisions yourself.

Lord, thank You for providing not only Your Word but solid examples of people who put Your Word into action. Help me to learn from their wisdom.

KEEP WATCH AND PRAY

And he cometh unto the disciples, and findeth them asleep, and saith unto Peter, What, could ye not watch with me one hour? Watch and pray, that ye enter not into temptation: the spirit indeed is willing, but the flesh is weak.
MATTHEW 26:40–41

Jesus never promised a life free of temptation and testing. Even men of unshakably strong faith will find themselves tempted to sin against the Lord. Jesus Himself—Son of the living God and God in the flesh—faced severe temptation at the beginning of His earthly ministry (Matthew 4:1–11).

Now, as He neared His final hours on earth, Jesus spoke words that apply to any man of God when He told His sleepy, emotionally exhausted disciples, "Watch and pray, that ye enter not into temptation."

Jesus' words speak this important wisdom into our lives: If we're going to fight a winning battle against sin and temptation, we're going to have to remain spiritually alert for temptation. . .and we'll need to pray for God's strength and wisdom.

Lord Jesus, like Your disciples, I find that my spirit is willing but my flesh is weak. May I always remain alert, pray continually, and rely on You in all ways to be strengthened in my faith.

SCRIPTURE INDEX

OLD TESTAMENT

Genesis

Exodus

Leviticus

Numbers

Deuteronomy

Joshua

Judges

1 Samuel

2 Samuel

Proverbs

Mark

Luke

John

Acts

Romans

MORE GREAT READING FOR MEN!

This powerful and practical guide is packed with invaluable information on scripture memorization. It lays out vital, need-to-know scriptures for your everyday life, plus much more—an overview of all 66 books of the Bible, helpful hints for retaining scripture, and a comprehensive list of Bible memory verses in biblical order.

Paperback / ISBN 979-8-89151-085-2